CW00336625

ACOUSTIC GUITAR MAGAZINE'S
private lessons

SWING GUITAR ESSENTIALS

STRING LETTER PUBLISHING

Publisher: David A. Lusterman

Editorial Director: Jeffrey Pepper Rodgers

Editor: Scott Nygaard

Managing Editor: Simone Solondz

Music Editor: Dylan Schorer

Designer: Gary Cribb

Production Coordinator: Christi Payne

Music Engraving: Dylan Schorer

Cover Photo: Rory Earnshaw

Photographs: Frank Driggs Collection (Freddie Green, Eddie Lang, Django Reinhardt, Bob Wills), Rory
Earnshaw (Dix Bruce), Anne Hamersky (Scott Nygaard), Susan Johannsen (Tony Marcus)

© 1999 published by String Letter Publishing, Inc.

David A. Lusterman, Publisher

ISBN 978-1-890490-18-8

Printed in the United States of America.

All rights reserved. This book was produced by String Letter Publishing, Inc.,

PO Box 767, San Anselmo, California 94979-0767; (415) 485-6946; www.acousticguitar.com

Library of Congress Cataloging-in-Publication Data

Swing guitar essentials.

     p. cm. – (Acoustic guitar magazine's private lessons)

  Includes discographies.

  ISBN 978-1-890490-18-8

  1. Guitar Methods (Swing) Self-instruction.   2. Swing (Music)–Instruction and study.

I. Series

MT588.S9 1999

787.87'1931654–dc21   99-26412

                                                     CIP

STRING LETTER PUBLISHING

contents

CD *track list*

introduction

Every so often, all musicians need to revisit the roots of contemporary music and reconsider the players who got us where we are today. Dipping into the well of older styles helps us to reconnect with essential qualities in music that are being neglected in the current scene, and in turn inspires the next round of invention. Looking to the past has been a major theme in the '90s, as players tune into prewar strains of acoustic blues, country

and mountain music, and the subject of this lesson book—swing music. Thanks in particular to bands like the Squirrel Nut Zippers, the Brian Setzer Orchestra, and Cherry Poppin' Daddies, swing fever has struck even such unlikely outposts as modern-rock radio and MTV. But so far, interest in this music has run way ahead of knowledge of its history and vital elements.

Swing is a slippery term that's used to define a type of rhythm, an entire era, and several styles of music. As far as the acoustic guitar goes, one of the most important—and least understood—styles of swing guitar was perfected by the unassuming rhythm guitarist for Count Basie's band, Freddie Green. Then there's Gypsy jazz, whose devotees have their own guitar hero, Django Reinhardt, their own signature instruments, Selmer guitars, and their own sizzling lead and rhythm style. Another strong current is western swing, pioneered by Bob Wills, and its offshoots such as Texas swing and cowboy swing. Along with a full lineup of lessons on swing guitar techniques and full songs to play, this book introduces you to these essential styles—the pioneering players and the instruments they favored, as well as must-hear recordings.

Start with the opening lessons and get some of the fundamental techniques under your fingers, then set off exploring these swing styles. Your guides are not only great teachers, but—as a spin of the CD will make clear—great players who do justice to the original sultans of swing.

Jeffrey Pepper Rodgers
Editor, *Acoustic Guitar*

music notation key

The music in this book is written in standard notation and tablature. Here's how to read it.

STANDARD NOTATION

Standard notation is written on a five-line staff. Notes are written in alphabetical order from A to G.

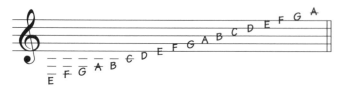

The duration of a note is determined by three things: the note head, stem, and flag. A whole note (○) equals four beats. A half note (♩) is half of that: two beats. A quarter note (♩) equals one beat, an eighth note (♪) equals half of one beat, and a 16th note (♪) is a quarter beat (there are four 16th notes per beat).

The fraction (4/4, 3/4, 6/8, etc.) or ¢ character shown at the beginning of a piece of music denotes the time signature. The top number tells you how many beats are in each measure, and the bottom number indicates the rhythmic value of each beat (4 equals a quarter note, 8 equals an eighth note, 16 equals a 16th note, and 2 equals a half note). The most common time signature is 4/4, which signifies four quarter notes per measure and is sometimes designated with the symbol ¢ (for common time). The symbol ¢ stands for cut time (2/2). Most songs are either in 4/4 or 3/4.

TABLATURE

In tablature, the six horizontal lines represent the six strings of the guitar, with the first string on the top and sixth on the bottom. The numbers refer to fret numbers on a given string. The notation and tablature in this book are designed to be used in tandem—refer to the notation to get the rhythmic information and note durations, and refer to the tablature to get the exact locations of the notes on the guitar fingerboard.

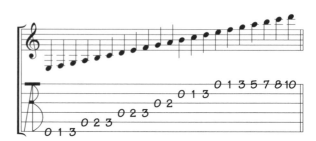

FINGERINGS

Fingerings are indicated with small numbers and letters in the notation. Fretting-hand fingering is indicated with 1 for the index finger, 2 the middle, 3 the ring, 4 the pinky, and *T* the thumb. Picking-hand fingering is indicated by *i* for the index finger, *m* the middle, *a* the ring, *c* the pinky, and *p* the thumb. Circled numbers indicate the string the note is played on. Remember that the fingerings indicated are only suggestions; if you find a different way that works better for you, use it.

CHORD DIAGRAMS

Chord diagrams show where the fingers go on the fingerboard. Frets are shown horizontally. The thick top line represents the nut. A Roman numeral to the right of a diagram indicates a chord played higher up the neck (in this case the top horizontal line is thin). Strings are shown as vertical lines. The line on the far left represents the sixth (lowest) string, and the line on the far right represents the first (highest) string. Dots show where the fingers go, and thick horizontal lines indicate barres. Numbers above the diagram are left-hand finger numbers, as used in standard notation. Again, the fingerings are only suggestions. An *X* indicates a string that should be muted or not played; 0 indicates an open string.

CAPOS

If a capo is used, a Roman numeral indicates the fret where the capo should be placed. The standard notation and tablature is written as if the capo were the nut of the guitar. For instance, a tune capoed anywhere up the neck and played using key-of-G chord shapes and fingerings will be written in the key of G. Likewise, open strings held down by the capo are written as open strings.

TUNINGS

Alternate guitar tunings are given from the lowest (sixth) string to the highest (first) string. For instance, D A D G B E indicates standard tuning with the bottom string dropped to D. Standard notation for songs in alternate tunings always reflects the actual pitches of the notes.

VOCAL TUNES

Vocal tunes are sometimes written with a fully tabbed-out introduction and a vocal melody with chord diagrams for the rest of the piece. The tab intro is usually your indication of which strum or fingerpicking pattern to use in the rest of the piece. The melody with lyrics underneath is the melody sung by the vocalist. Occasionally, smaller notes are written with the melody to indicate the harmony part sung by another vocalist. These are not to be confused with cue notes, which are small notes that indicate melodies that vary when a section is repeated. Listen to a recording of the piece to get a feel for the guitar accompaniment and to hear the singing if you aren't skilled at reading vocal melodies.

ARTICULATIONS

There are a number of ways you can articulate a note on the guitar. Notes connected with slurs (not to be confused with ties) in the tablature or standard notation are articulated with either a hammer-on, pull-off, or slide. Lower notes slurred to higher notes are played as hammer-ons; higher notes slurred to lower notes are played as pull-offs. While it's usually obvious that slurred notes are played as hammer-ons or pull-offs, an *H* or *P* is included above the tablature as an extra reminder.

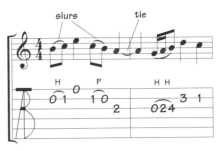

Slides are represented with a dash, and an *S* is included above the tab. A dash preceding a note represents a slide into the note from an indefinite point in the direction of the slide; a dash following a note indicates a slide off of the note to an indefinite point in the direction of the slide. For two slurred notes connected with a slide, you should pick the first note and then slide into the second.

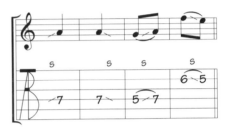

Bends are represented with upward curves, as shown in the next example. Most bends have a specific destination pitch—the number above the bend symbol shows how much the bend raises the string's pitch: ¼ for a slight bend, ½ for a half step, 1 for a whole step.

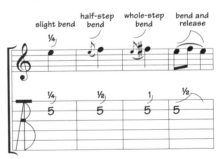

Grace notes are represented by small notes with a dash through the stem in standard notation and with small numbers in the tab. A grace note is a very quick ornament leading into a note, most commonly executed as a hammer-on, pull-off, or slide. In the first example below, pluck the note at the fifth fret on the beat, then quickly hammer onto the seventh fret. The second example is executed as a quick pull-off from the second fret to the open string. In the third example, both notes at the fifth fret are played simultaneously (even though it appears that the fifth fret, fourth string, is to be played by itself), then the seventh fret, fourth string, is quickly hammered.

HARMONICS

Harmonics are represented by diamond-shaped notes in the standard notation and a small dot next to the tablature numbers. Natural harmonics are indicated with the text "Harmonics" or "Harm." above the tablature. Harmonics articulated with the right hand (often called artificial harmonics) include the text "R.H. Harmonics" or "R.H. Harm." above the tab. Right-hand harmonics are executed by lightly touching the harmonic node (usually 12 frets above the open string or fretted note) with the right-hand index finger and plucking the string with the thumb or ring finger or pick. For extended phrases played with right-hand harmonics, the fretted notes are shown in the tab along with instructions to touch the harmonics 12 frets above the notes.

REPEATS

One of the most confusing parts of a musical score can be the navigation symbols, such as repeats, *D.S. al Coda*, *D.C. al Fine*, *To Coda*, etc.

Repeat symbols are placed at the beginning and end of the passage to be repeated.

You should ignore repeat symbols with the dots on the right side the first time you encounter them; when you come to a repeat symbol with dots on the left side, jump back to the previous repeat symbol facing the opposite direction (if there is no previous symbol, go to the beginning of the piece). The next time you come to the repeat symbol, ignore it and keep going unless it includes instructions such as "Repeat three times."

A section will often have a different ending after each repeat. The example below includes a first and a second ending. Play until you hit the repeat symbol, jump back to the previous repeat symbol and play until you reach the bracketed first ending, skip the measures under the bracket and jump immediately to the second ending, and then continue.

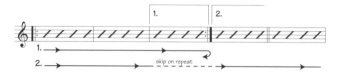

D.S. stands for *dal segno* or "from the sign." When you encounter this indication, jump immediately to the sign (𝄋). *D.S.* is usually accompanied by *al Fine* or *al Coda*. *Fine* indicates the end of a piece. *A coda* is a final passage near the end of a piece and is indicated with ⊕. *D.S. al Coda* simply tells you to jump back to the sign and continue on until you are instructed to jump to the coda, indicated with *To Coda* ⊕.

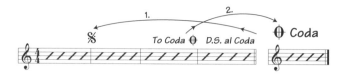

D.C. stands for *da capo* or "from the beginning." Jump to the top of the piece when you encounter this indication.

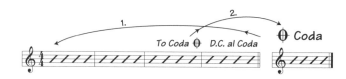

D.C. al Fine tells you to jump to the beginning of a tune and continue until you encounter the *Fine* indicating the end of the piece (ignore the *Fine* the first time through).

about the teachers

DIX BRUCE

Writer and musician Dix Bruce has been playing guitar for over 30 years and teaching for 25. He has released two albums with guitarist Jim Nunally, *From Fathers to Sons* and *The Way Things Are,* and two solo CDs, *My Folk Heart* and *Tuxedo Blues: String Swing and Jazz* (all on Musix, PO Box 231005, Pleasant Hill, CA 94523). He has also written 30 instructional books, including *Rounder Old-Time Music for Guitar, Doc Watson and Clarence Ashley: 1960–1962, You Can Teach Yourself Country Guitar,* and *Backup Trax* (all from Mel Bay).

HAL GLATZER

Writer and swing rhythm guitar player Hal Glatzer divides his time between San Francisco and New York City. An enthusiast for the aesthetics as well as the music of the 1920s, '30s, and '40s, he collects sheet music, vintage artifacts, and ephemera. He has written extensively about the computer industry, acoustic music, commercial graphic arts, and home-office improvements and is currently writing a mystery series.

DAVID HAMBURGER

David Hamburger is a guitarist, teacher, and writer who lives in Brooklyn, New York. He has played guitar, Dobro, and pedal steel on numerous recordings, including Chuck Brodsky's *Radio* (Red House, 1998), Salamander Crossing's *Passion Train* (Signature Sounds, 1996), and his own 1994 debut recording on Chester Records, *King of the Brooklyn Delta* (www.songs.com/hamburski). His most recent instructional book is *The Dobro Workbook* (Hal Leonard, 1998).

JOHN JORGENSON

John Jorgenson is probably best known for his stellar guitar and mandolin playing with Chris Hillman and the Desert Rose Band or with Jerry Donohue and Will Ray in the Hellecasters. Most of Jorgenson's work has been in the world of country and rock, but it is Gypsy jazz that is closest to his heart. In 1988 Jorgenson recorded his solo debut *After You've Gone* (Curb), a charming collection of swing standards and original tunes. Jorgenson is currently playing guitar with Elton John and has released *Emotional Savant* (J2/Pharaoh), a solo CD featuring his vocals and lyrics in a rock format, and *Crop Circles* (Solid Air), an album of original instrumental duets with guitarist Davey Johnstone. He is currently recording the follow-up to *After You've Gone.* Visit Jorgenson on the Web at www.hellecasters.com.

JOHN LEHMANN-HAUPT

John Lehmann-Haupt has recorded his arrangements of popular and traditional songs on the Physical World label and selections from his classical repertoire for the AIG Records Guitar Masters series. He has been on the teaching staff of New York's American Institute of Guitar since 1982, and he has written extensively on music and the guitar for *The New York Times* and several magazines.

TONY MARCUS

Tony Marcus plays lead guitar and violin in '30s and '40s swing band Cats and Jammers, which records for the Tuxedo label (2557 Wakefield Ave., Oakland, CA 94606). He's also played with the Arkansas Sheiks, the Cheap Suit Serenaders (featuring counter-culture cartoonist Robert Crumb), and the Royal Society Jazz Orchestra.

SCOTT NYGAARD

Acoustic Guitar magazine's associate editor, Scott Nygaard is an accomplished guitarist with more than 25 years' experience. He has performed and recorded with such artists as Laurie Lewis and Grant Street, Tim O'Brien and the O'Boys, and Jerry Douglas and has released two albums, *No Hurry* and *Dreamer's Waltz,* both on Rounder. He has had many articles and lessons published in *Acoustic Guitar* magazine.

MICHAEL SIMMONS

Michael Simmons plays guitar and ukulele. He has been playing musette and jazz Manouche for the last decade. When he was nine years old he tried to run away with the Gypsies but they brought him home. He currently works at Gryphon Stringed Instruments in Palo Alto, California.

Jazz Chord Basics

Dix Bruce

The term *jazz chord* conjures up confusion and mystery for many guitarists. The fingerings are unfamiliar, and technical terms such as *major seven, seven flat nine, dominant seven suspended with a sharp 11,* and *diminished* (I've heard this referred to as "demented") are enough to scare anyone off for years. Add to that the perceived difficulty of playing these chords all over the neck and you've got a strong enough excuse to avoid them for the rest of your life.

On the other hand, jazz chords offer the guitarist a vastly expanded palette of tonal colors and entry into an unlimited universe of modern music, including pop, rock, and classical. And if you want to play swing or jazz, they're essential.

The good news is that once you get into these types of chords, you'll find a system that is logical, regular, and easy to use. The trick is to discover a bridge from what you know to what you don't know. In this lesson, we'll make that bridge out of the blues by looking at the chords to a simple blues riff, the kind that players as diverse as Louis Armstrong, Benny Goodman, Bob Wills, Django Reinhardt, Thelonious Monk, John Coltrane, Charlie Christian, Joe Pass, Wynton Marsalis, and George Benson have all composed, played, and recorded. We'll learn some basic closed-position chords and discuss how to move them around. In the process, we'll transpose our blues riff from the key of G to the key of B♭.

Musically speaking, there is no such thing as a "jazz chord," any more than there are special cubist colors for painters or designated mystery words for writers. A chord is a chord, and jazz chords are often just basic chords played in unfamiliar forms and positions on the fretboard, or extended or altered versions of these same basic chords. The former can include chords played up the neck in closed positions, which are sometimes called barre chords. These chords don't utilize open strings; each note is fretted. Extended chords have notes—the nines, 11s, 13s, etc.—added to basic triads (chords with three notes). Altered chords have one or more notes changed, as in flatted fives or sharp nines.

The main emphasis here is on closed-position and barre chords. If you've tried them on an acoustic guitar, especially one with high action, you know how difficult they can be to play correctly without buzzes or unintentionally muted notes.

One of the reasons we use closed-position chords is that they can be moved up and down the neck. Knowing this, you can learn chords by form and move these forms anywhere. A chord then becomes, for example, a *dominant seven form* rather than, say, merely a G7 chord. Most chord forms can be played in at least 12 different places on the fretboard.

Here's an example: The chord on the left below is the familiar form of the G7 chord that uses open strings. The 0's above the grid denote strings played open. The chord on the right is a closed-position dominant seven form played at the third fret. It's also a G7. With this form, the first and fifth strings are muted; the X's above the grid show which strings do not sound.

Jazz chords offer the guitarist a vastly expanded palette of tonal colors.

Introduction

The open form is not movable, and we'd have to learn a totally different form for an F7 or a B♭7 chord. By contrast, the closed form is movable and yields a new chord at every fret. Move it down two frets and it's an F7. Move it up to the sixth fret and it's a B♭7.

Closed-position chords also allow you to control the rhythmic sound of the strum with the fretting hand by loosening the grip between strums just enough to mute all the sound from the strings. This creates a rhythmic pulse, usually called a *comp,* that reinforces the groove and swing of the chords played in swing and jazz as well as in blues, rock, and country music. If you have open strings in the chord, you can't easily shut off the sound like this.

A riff blues is made up of a repeating lick played over blues chord changes, in this case with a 12-measure form. You'll find this basic chord progression in thousands of tunes played all over the world. The riff blues you'll learn here is presented in three versions of varying difficulty. The first version is in G, and the other two are in B♭. All use only closed-position chords. Each could be played with simple open-position chords, but open chords won't allow easy transposition up and down the neck or let you play the comp mentioned above.

The chords in "Blues in G" are all dominant seven chords, which consist of a basic triad with the flatted seventh of the chord's major scale added. They're usually just called seventh chords. Here's a very brief explanation.

The G-major scale looks like this:

G	A	B	C	D	E	F♯	G
Do	Re	Mi	Fa	Sol	La	Ti	Do
1	2	3	4	5	6	7	8

A G-major triad is made up of the 1, 3, and 5 notes of the G-major scale, as shown in this chord diagram.

Even though we're playing six notes, we're really only playing three *different* notes: G, B, and D, which are the 1, 3, and 5 of the G-major scale. If we add the flatted seven of the G-major scale, the F♮ note, to this basic G triad, we'll end up with a G dominant seven chord. (The seven of the G scale is an F♯. Flatting the note lowers it one half step to an F♮.)

Every chord has a unique recipe, and a chord's name reflects the scale tones it includes. In the process of learning a chord system, you'll identify how each chord form supplies the correct ingredient chord tones and learn how to apply each in a variety of different situations. The chord forms in this riff blues are from a collection of "orchestral" chords commonly played in big bands in the 1930s and '40s. They're big, beefy chords, and they're great for swing and traditional jazz. Most are four-string chords with muted first or fifth strings. In the chord diagrams below, each form can be identified by determining which chord tone is in the bass. The first chord shown is a dominant seven form with the 1 or root in the bass. Since this is a G7 chord, the bass note is a G. The second form is a dominant seven with the fifth in the bass. Since this is a C7, the bass note is G. The third form is the same as the second, only two frets higher. In this D7, the fifth or bass note is an A.

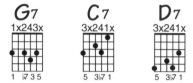

Take some time to learn these forms. If you're new to playing closed-position chords, be advised that it takes a while to build up the strength in your fretting hand so you can play them cleanly and up to speed.

To get the required swing feel, start by setting up a rhythm pattern, all downstrokes, made up of four even strums in each measure. Once you can do that, try damping each strum a split second after you sound it and before you play the next one by loosening your fretting hand's grip just enough to stop the sound without creating buzzes.

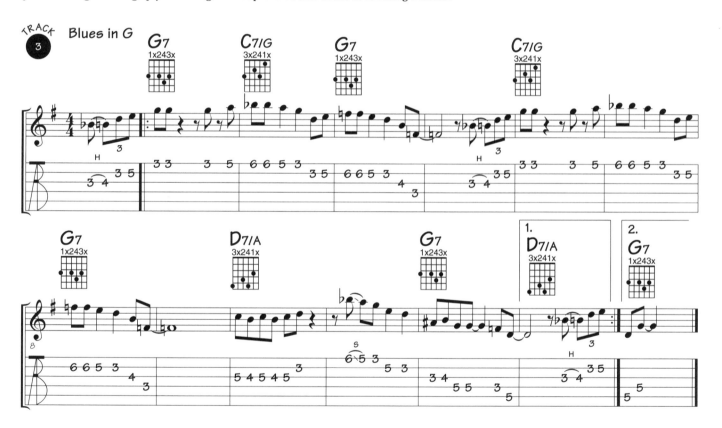

After you've mastered the chords, try learning the melody, which, just like the chords, is written in the tablature in a closed and thus movable form.

Now let's move this whole tune up three frets (or a minor third) to the key of B♭. Try doing this in your head. Close your eyes and picture the chords you just learned at their new position. After you move your fretting hand up, everything will be the same, just higher on the neck. If you have problems, look at the chord grids. Chord charts are quite different from standard music and tablature. The first thing you'll notice is that there's no written melody. Instead, there are slashes like this (/ / / /), four to a measure, which represent the four strums/beats in each measure. The chords and their positions are written above the measures. Don't forget to try playing your riffs in B♭.

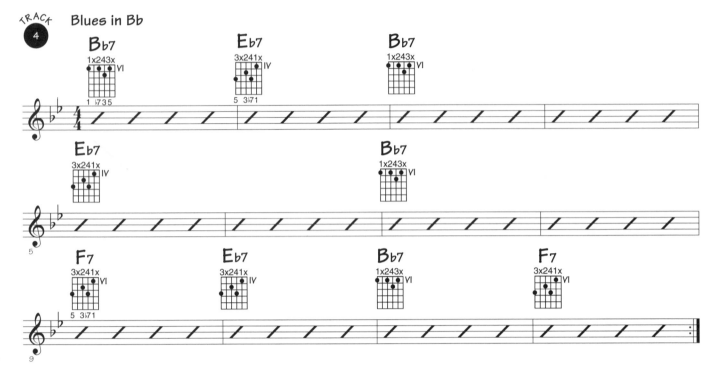

Once you can play the first version of "Blues in B♭," try number two, with several new chord forms. These changes are typical of a standard 12-bar jazz blues, with many chords played for only two beats/strums (note the first four measures). This gives the tune a kind of forward motion. The first measure begins with a new movable B♭ chord that uses all six strings and the first finger as a barre. (The alternate fingering shown in the first chord diagram has the thumb instead of the first finger acting as the barre.) The first time it appears, each chord is diagrammed below its grid to show where each part of the chord lies: 1, 3, 5, ♭7, etc.

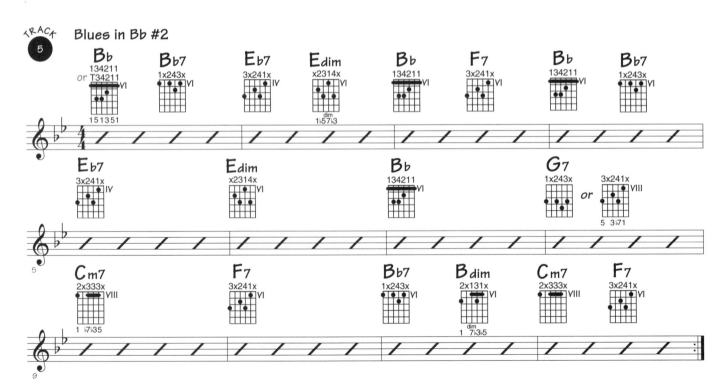

The E diminished chord in measure 2, sometimes notated with a small open circle (o), uses a different string set than most of the other chords. In this case you mute strings one and six. The "dim 7" notation under the third string of the grid means "diminished seven," and this note is one half step lower than the flatted seven note. The natural seven of the E-major scale is a D♯, so the flatted seven is D♮. Lower it one more half step to D♭. Measure 11 uses another diminished form; this one, like the dominant sevens from "Blues in G," mutes the first and fifth strings. The G7 in measure 8 is shown with a familiar alternate. Any G7 chord form, even the open-string G7, can be substituted here. Get in the habit of figuring out different voicings to substitute even though your fretting hand may be jumping from the third fret to the eighth fret. Ultimately you'll want to avoid these big jumps, but for now, experiment to learn where all the chords are. What other dominant seven form can you substitute for the given first chord in measure 2? The C minor seven (Cm7) in measure 9 is another "orchestral" chord with muted first and fifth strings. The root is in the bass, as you can see from the diagram, and the chord is made up of the notes C, E♭, G, and B♭, which are the 1, ♭3, 5, and ♭7 of the C-major scale. Finally, measures 11 and 12 make up what is called a turnaround. These chords are meant to turn the progression back to the beginning for another time through. If you were ending the tune, you could hold a B♭ chord through both measures. Musicians often play the chords used in the turnaround as a repeating "vamp" to begin a tune or kill time before the singer comes in.

Memorize all the chords and concentrate on keeping a groove, no matter how slow or fast you play. Once you can play the B♭ versions, bump everything up two more frets to the key of C. Don't stop there—move farther up the neck and then back down again. This type of transposing practice is the most important thing you can do to teach yourself how these chords work.

MASTERS OF SWING RHYTHM

It's difficult to describe on paper the rhythmic pulse or comp you need to play in this style. Listening to just about any big-band swing guitarist from the 1930s or '40s will give you an idea of what to shoot for. This can be a frustrating exercise because it's often difficult to hear clearly what the rhythm guitarist is doing above the sound of the rest of the band. Your best chance of identifying the sound is on slower tunes behind vocals or piano solos. Listen closely (you may need headphones) to **Freddie Green with Count Basie.** There are three or four cuts, including "Hey, Pretty Baby," on *Basie's Basement* (Bluebird/RCA 61065), where Green's very subtle magic is evident. Charlie Christian's rhythm can occasionally be heard with the Benny Goodman Sextet (Benny Goodman Sextet, *Featuring Charlie Christian,* Columbia 45144; **Charlie Christian,** *The Genius of the Electric Guitar,* Columbia 40846). Of course Christian's historic, exciting, and brilliant lead playing is always right up front and featured. **Django Reinhardt**'s recordings with the Quintet of the Hot Club of France have very prominent rhythm guitar, often with two rhythm guitarists behind the leads. The Hot Club rhythm style is, well, "hot": on top of the beat, not as laid back as the bluesier Basie/Green style. Duet records by **George Barnes** and **Carl Kress** are great for hearing two different styles of comping, as each guitarist backs up the other. A favorite recording of mine, with very clear—though more modern—comping, is Kress and Barnes' *Two Guitars* (Jass 636). Also recommended are recordings by the **Ruby Braff/George Barnes Quartet,** which was drummerless and included an acoustic rhythm guitarist, and *Basie Jam 2* (Pablo 631) with Joe Pass.

Movable Chord Forms

Dix Bruce

Learning one chord position allows you to play 12 different chords.

Introduction

As you evolve as a musician, you'll find that most pop, rock, and jazz tunes are based on only a handful of chord progressions. Recognizing these progressions in unfamiliar songs will instantly give you clues on how to play chord accompaniment and lead lines. Let's continue to explore these movable, closed-position chords and apply them to a typical set of swing/jazz chord changes. We'll analyze how these chords function in keys, identify recurring patterns in a song's chord progression, and learn a few new chord positions and a new melody.

Keep in mind that "jazz chords" are simply closed-position chords that can be moved up and down the neck. For example, the same chord form produces a D♭7 if you play it at the second fret, a D7 at the third fret, and an E♭7 at the fourth fret.

Basic closed-position, three-tone chords, or triads, like G, B♭, F, Am, and Em, can be moved up and down the neck, as can more extended or altered chords, such as Cmaj7, Daug, Gm7(♭5), and E♭9(♭13). The great advantage to understanding this approach is that learning one chord position allows you to play 12 different chords.

INVERSIONS

You can also play different inversions of the same chord. For example, a four-string D7 chord can be played at four different positions on the neck, with the notes played in a different order in each one. The first form shown below has the fifth of the chord in the bass (sixth string), the second has the flatted seventh in the bass, the third has its root in the bass, and the last one (a somewhat impractical form at this high neck position) has its third in the bass.

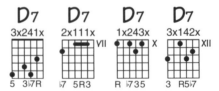

There are two reasons why a guitarist would want to know four different D7 chords at various fretboard positions. First, each position offers a slightly different sound. Second, knowing how to play a given chord in several different regions of the fretboard can help you avoid unnecessary hand movement.

Let's say, for example, that you're playing a song with the chord progression D7, G7, C. Suppose you begin with the D7 (shown above) played at the tenth fret. Next comes G7 and

C. You probably know forms for these chords that are way down near the other end of the neck, which would make for a huge jump with your fretting hand. It would be much easier to play G7 and C forms in the same neighborhood on your fretboard as the D7. Try these:

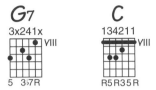

We can identify most songs in pop and jazz by their chord progressions. For example, thousands of simple folk, country, and rock songs use only two or three chords, usually the I (one), the IV (four), and the V (five). These chord numbers come from the major scales that define each key. The F-major scale is:

F	G	A	B♭	C	D	E	F
Do	Re	Mi	Fa	Sol	La	Ti	Do
1	2	3	4	5	6	7	8

The chords derived from the F-major scale are:

F	Gm	Am	B♭	C	Dm	Edim
I	ii	iii	IV	V	vi	vii

Notice that we identify notes in a scale with Arabic numerals and chords in a key with Roman numerals, and that uppercase Roman numerals represent major chords and lowercase represent minors.

A song with the chord progression I–IV–V–I in the key of F would use the chords F, B♭, C, and F. If you know chords in other keys by their corresponding numbers, transposition to any other key is a snap. I–IV–V–I in the key of C would use the chords C, F, G, and C. Another type of song might have I–V–I on the verse and IV–I–V–I for the chorus. Songs described as "blues changes" would have chords similar to this: I–IV–I–I7–IV–I–VI7–II7–V7–I. Those chords in the key of Bb would be: B♭, E♭, B♭, B♭7, E♭, B♭, G7, C7, F7, B♭. What would they be in the key of F? A minor blues would be something like this: i–iv–i–iv–i–V–i. What would these chords be in the key of F?

CYCLE OF FIFTHS PROGRESSIONS

Another very popular chord progression is the I–VI–II–V. Notice that the VI and II chords are major. In practice, they would actually be played as dominant seventh chords (which are always major), like the D7 shown above. Some players refer to this as a "dominant turnaround"; others might call it a "cycle of fifths." Progressions with minor chords sound quite different from those with dominant sevenths, but the I–VI–II–V label is applied to both. Substitute one for the other in a familiar song and listen to the difference.

There are literally thousands of songs in the pop and jazz worlds built at least in part on the I–VI–II–V progression, including "Salty Dog," "Don't Let Your Deal Go Down," and "Sweet Georgia Brown." There are thousands more that add a III chord to make a I–III–VI–II–V pattern, including "All of Me," "Five Foot Two," and "On the Sunny Side of the Street." A song may combine two or more different progressions. The trick to identifying the progressions is to look at a song in the context of its home key and try to relate the changes to a pattern.

I wrote "Dominant Seven Swing" in the key of F with chord moves similar to the song "Sweet Georgia Brown." The melody is based on a repetitive jazz riff. Notice that we can play the same basic riff on the G7 that was played on the D7 by simply lowering the F♯ notes to F♮. The melody over the C7 is simply the D7 melody moved down one step. The rest of the melody sticks close to the chord tones, with some chromatic passing tones tossed in for melodic interest.

Look at each of the chords in the song and compare it to the key-of-F chords listed on page 17. The correct number designations for the chords are: D7 = VI, G7 = II, C7 = V, F = I, A7 = III, and Dm = vi. We thus have a VI–II–V–I pattern in the first 15 measures (which would actually be referred to as I–VI–II–V–I). In the 16th measure, a III chord brings us to a VI–II pattern through measure 24. In measures 25–28, we have two Dm–A7 (vi–III) changes, and the last four bars are another I–VI–II–V–I progression.

Except for the I chord, a typical dominant I–VI–II–V–I progression is made up of all dominant chords, which is simply another term for chords like D7, G7, C7, and F7—major triads with the flatted seventh note added. To make the G dominant seventh chord, we take the 1, 3, and 5 notes of the G-major scale (G, B, and D) and add the flatted 7 (F♯). These are the notes that make up a G7 chord.

Chord diagrams for "Dominant Seven Swing" are shown below. The numbers below each chord diagram show which part of the chord each string supplies (the root note is identified with an *R*). Notice which note of the chord is in the bass. In the first C7 chord, the fifth is on string six, the *X* tells us that string five is muted, string four has the third of the chord, string three has the flatted seventh, string two has the root, and string one is muted.

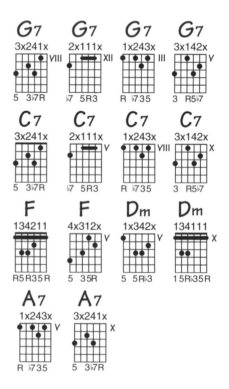

The chord forms used in the first 15 measures of the song are all played in the lower region of the fretboard. The A7 in measure 16 is a bit of a jump, but it's used as a transition to the upper part of the fretboard and another group of forms. Usually you'd opt to play the entire song in one region of the fretboard, but this arrangement will help famil-

Dominant Seven Swing

Music by Dix Bruce

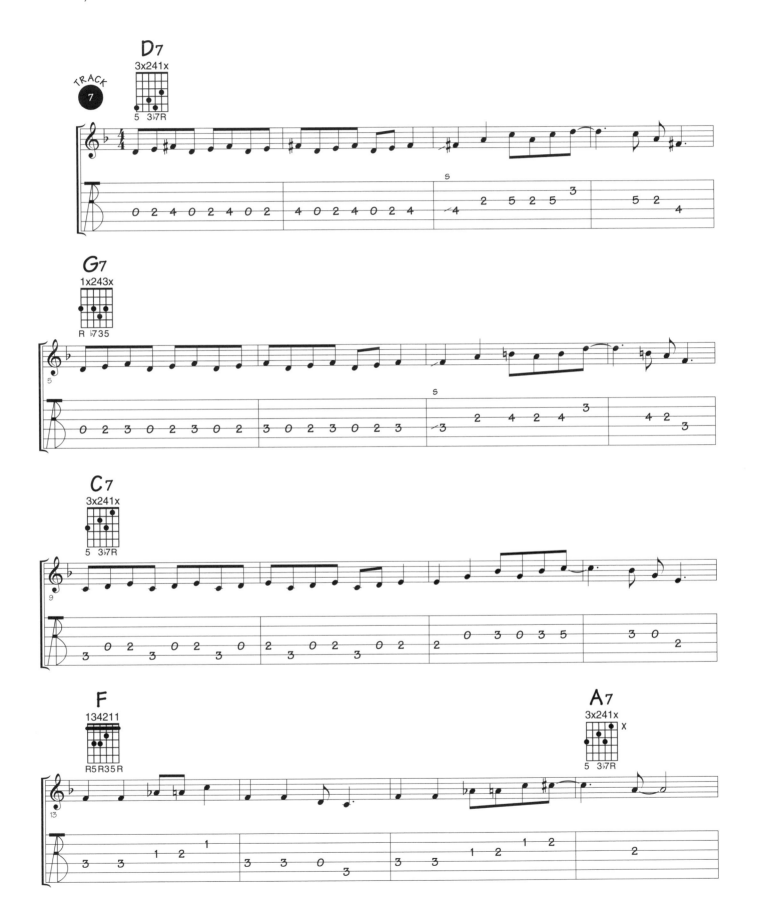

iarize you with different regions. You could certainly substitute the A7 form with the root in the bass, playing it at the fifth fret.

As you work through the song and memorize the chords, it's important that you keep a good steady rhythm or "comp" going with your strumming hand. To play the swing or jazz comp in a 4/4 tune like this, strum the chord and then relax the fretting hand to cut off the sound. Put more emphasis on the backbeats of each measure: 1 2 3 4. The result is an even and swinging pulse or groove. The muted strings in these chords can sometimes present a problem; they may ring or buzz when they shouldn't. You can eventually eliminate this problem by adjusting the position of your fretting hand slightly after each strum.

It may take you weeks or months to teach your head and hands to play these chords cleanly. Don't whip through the easy chords and slow down on the tough ones. Remember, it don't mean a thing if it ain't got that swing.

Once you can play the song's chords as written, move the whole set of forms up and down the neck one fret at a time to transpose the song into different keys. The melody as written uses open strings and is thus not movable, so you'll need to work it out in a closed position to transpose it. Next, go back to the original key of F and challenge yourself by substituting the other forms shown for each chord. You'll notice that there are only two A7 chord forms shown. See if you can figure out how and where to best play the A7 with the different forms of the other dominant seven chords. Try to stay within three or four frets as you change chords so your fretting hand doesn't have to make any big jumps.

Understanding Swing Chord Progressions

David Hamburger

Introduction **TRACK 8**

Swing chord progressions can look a little bewildering to anyone accustomed to the simple verities of country, blues, or bluegrass. But like most things musical, you can create some order out of the chaos by learning how to categorize the tunes you encounter.

Swing tunes are usually 32 bars long and they usually can be categorized as either AABA or ABAC. In an AABA tune, the first melody (or A section) is eight bars long and is played twice, followed by a contrasting section referred to as the bridge (the B section), which is also eight bars long. The bridge is followed by a repeat of the first melody. In an ABAC tune, the B and C sections are often quite similar, and it can feel as if you're playing a 16-bar tune twice, with the B and C sections functioning as first and second endings to the A section.

Swing chords often change at a rate of two per bar. Just as you arrive, it's time to move on to the next chord. Understanding how these fast-moving chords relate to each other can help you see the music in units bigger than two beats at a time, which in turn makes it easier to hear what's going on, to remember how the chords go, and to actually play the music.

Let's start with a simple eight-bar section made up of just I, IV, and V chords in the key of G.

TRACK 9 Ex. 1

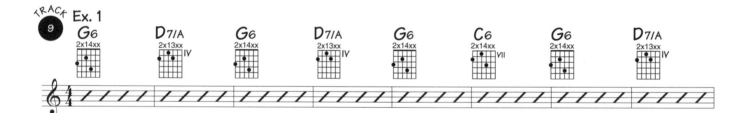

Simple enough, right? Now, let's take each measure of D and turn it into two beats of A minor and two beats of D. A minor is the ii chord in the key of G, so so you can add it in to create more motion in the harmony.

TRACK 10 Ex. 2

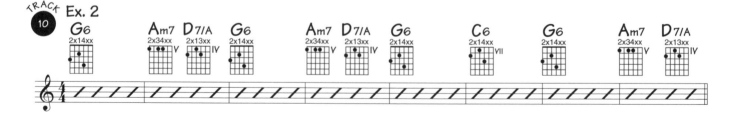

Next, let's lead into each A minor chord with an E7. E7 doesn't belong in the key of G, but it's the V chord of A minor. In other words, if you were in the key of A, your V chord would be E7. This is often referred to as a "borrowed chord" because we're borrowing E7 from another key. The E7 sounds cool because when you land on the A minor, your ear says, "Oh, OK. Now I see where you were heading with that weird E7 that doesn't belong in the key of G." We end up with this chord progression:

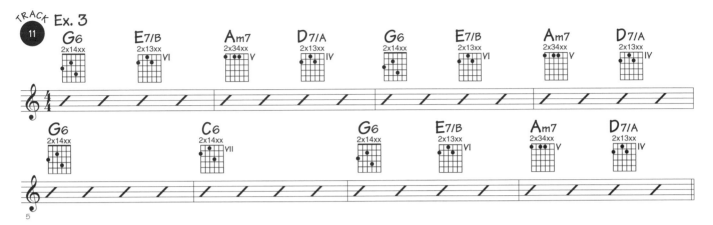

Finally, to smooth everything out, let's add two more chords in measures 5 and 6. In measure 5, we can play an inversion of G6 for the second two beats, and in measure 6 we can play two beats of C#dim, whose C# and A# notes move chromatically into the D and B notes of the G6 in measure 7.

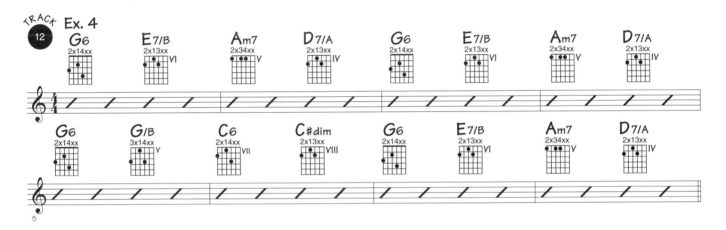

This eight-bar section is the A section to George and Ira Gershwin's 1930s tune "I Got Rhythm." This tune has been as popular as the blues form among swing and jazz musicians, and hundreds of melodies have been written to fit these chords. If you suggest jamming on some "rhythm changes," any self-respecting hipster will know just what you mean ("rhythm changes" is shorthand for "the chords to 'I Got Rhythm'"). Like the blues, you can play rhythm changes in any key, although the most common keys are B♭ and F, which are favorites for horn players.

Look at this eight-bar progression in the key of F:

C7	C7	C7	C7	F	B♭	F	D7
////	////	////	////	////	////	////	////

Pretty straightforward, right? All I's, IV's, and V's, except at the end. What's that D7 doing in there? Well, if we dress this progression up just a little, we'll end up with the chords to the A section to Fats Waller's "Honeysuckle Rose."

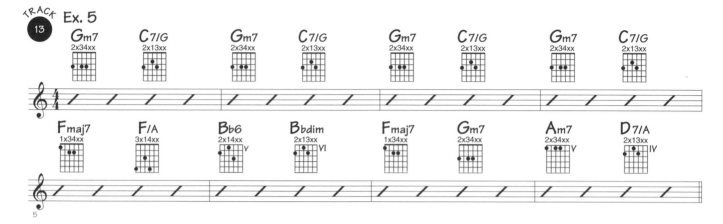

Every new chord has a reason, just like in "I Got Rhythm": G minor is the ii chord in the key of F, and all those G minors help keep things rocking back and forth every two beats instead of just sitting on the V chord for four whole bars. A minor is the iii chord in the key of F, but it's also the ii chord in the key of G minor, which leads into the D7, the V of G minor.

So if these are A sections, where are the B sections? The bridge to "I Got Rhythm" is as distinctive as its A section.

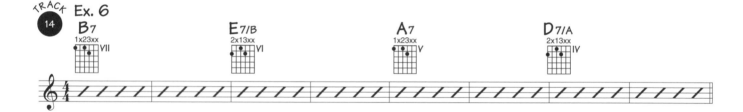

Talk about borrowed chords! The only chord that belongs in the key of G here is the D7. A7 is the V of D7, E7 is the V of A7, and B7 is the V of E7. So starting from the very first measure, this entire eight-bar progression is a chain of V chords, each one resolving to the next one until you get back to G. A sequence of chords like this is referred to as a cycle or circle of fifths because every chord is an interval of a fifth above the one that follows.

"Honeysuckle Rose" has a bridge made up of dominant chords, too, but it doesn't have as many borrowed chords. The F7 is the V of B♭ and the G7 is the V of C7.

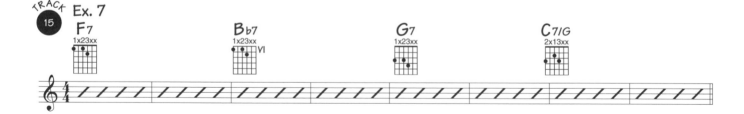

When you put these B sections together with their A sections to create an AABA form, you get the chord progressions for "I Got Rhythm" (Example 8) and "Honeysuckle Rose" (Example 9). There are countless AABA tunes, many of them similar to these two. Once you can recognize a tune as having this form and can see how the various chords relate to one another and to the basic I–IV–V skeleton of the chord progression, you'll have come a long way toward demystifying the situation.

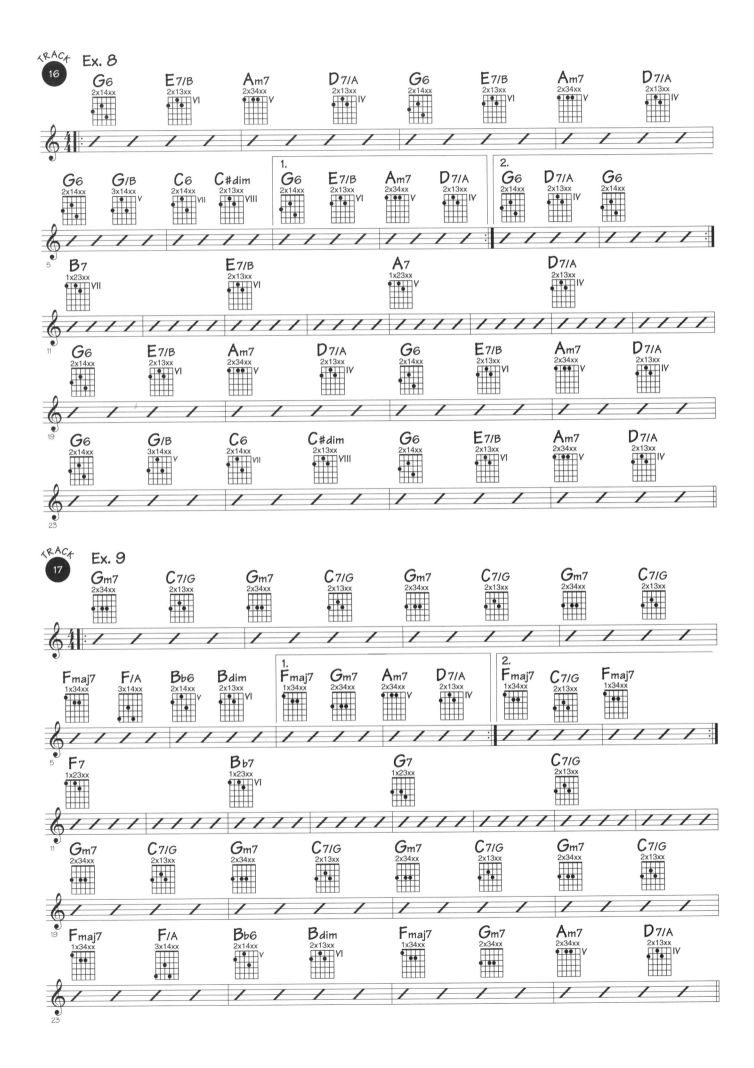

Finally, let's take a look at the ABAC tune "All of Me." In this case, the chords change about once every two bars until the C section. As you can see, the first and third lines are identical, while the second and fourth lines are different from both the first and third lines and from each other. See if you can figure out which chords are leading where and why, and then check your answers below.

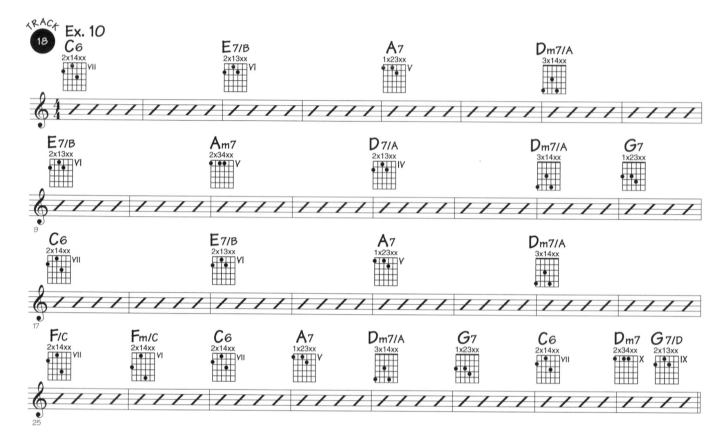

E7 is the V of A7, which is the V of D minor, which is the ii chord in the key of C. In the B section, D7 is the V of G7, which is the V in the key of C. F minor is there in the C section because it sounds good! The A♭ and the F notes resolve with contrary motion into the A♮ and E notes of the C6 chord.

Beginning Chord Melody

Dix Bruce

laying chord melody is a way to harmonize melody notes with chords. Whether you're strumming, flatpicking, or fingerpicking, playing guitar, banjo, or mandolin, the trick is to have the melody stand out above the chords.

Though this technique can be used in just about any style of guitar playing, from classical to country to rock to jazz, these days it is known primarily as a jazz guitar technique. Most of the great jazz guitarists, past and present (including Django Reinhardt, Barney Kessel, Herb Ellis, Wes Montgomery, Joe Pass, Tuck Andress, and Stanley Jordan), play their own versions of chord melody in both solo and ensemble situations.

The roots of jazz-guitar chord melody can be found in traditional and New Orleans–style jazz banjo playing of the 1920s. Many of the great early jazz guitarists, including Django Reinhardt, began their careers as banjo players and brought banjo techniques with them when they switched to guitar.

GETTING STARTED

Here are three simple examples of how to play chord melody on the first four measures of "Jingle Bells," where all the melody notes are played on the first and second strings. Example 1 shows chords being played on every beat. But you don't *have* to play a chord on every melody note. In fact, guitarists usually mix single notes and chords for melodic interest.

Most of the great jazz guitarists, past and present, play their own versions of chord melody.

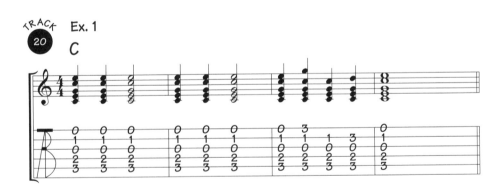

TRACK 20 **Ex. 1**
C

Introduction **TRACK 19**

In Example 2, chords are played on beats 1 and 3, single notes on beats 2 and 4.

TRACK 21 **Ex. 2**
C

Of course, there can be an infinite number of variations within the technique, especially with the use of chord extensions and substitutions. Example 3 shows one more variation on "Jingle Bells," with descending bass notes that essentially function as chord variations. There's also an additional V chord (G) on beat 4 of the third measure.

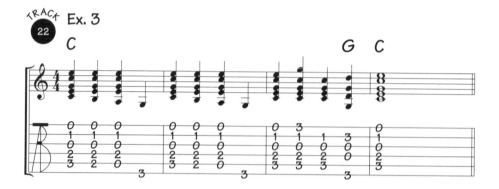

Let's build a chord melody solo for the old pop standard "Avalon," composed in 1920 by Vincent Rose, Al Jolson, and B.G. DeSylva. I chose this tune because it's a special favorite of mine and because the melody is composed almost entirely of half notes, which makes it work well as a simple chord melody. Quarter notes and eighth notes demand much faster chord switching.

Familiarize yourself with the simple, key-of-F version of "Avalon" on page 29 by playing through the melody and chord progression a few times. It's important that you have the simple melody and accompaniment in your mind and fingers before you move on to the chord melody. In the original sheet music, the melody is written an octave lower. I've raised it an octave so it will fall mostly on the first (highest) two strings of the guitar. First try playing the melody as shown in the tablature and then see if you can move it to different positions on the guitar's neck.

When you look at the full chord melody on page 30, you may at first feel overwhelmed; there are a lot of chords. But as you look more closely, you'll see that many of the later chords are simple repetitions of previous ones, identical chord forms moved up or down the neck, or familiar chord forms with a different first- or second-string melody note added. For example, the first chord is a C9 with a G note on the first string. The same chord is played on beats 3 and 4 of measure 3, and beats 1 and 2 of measure 4. In the second full measure, we have a Gm7 chord form on the first two beats. To play the chord shown for the second two beats, we simply add the fourth finger to the first string at the eighth fret. If you play the Am7♭5 from the first two beats of measure 18 two frets lower, you have the Gm7♭5 of measure 23. Analyze the chords to find identical forms, extensions, and altered chords, and try to identify how the chords function in the progression rather than merely memorizing them as separate and unrelated finger moves.

The chord notation used here is standard with one exception. Chords with an added tone, the melody note, are identified with an extra letter in parentheses. In measure 2 you'll find the Gm7(C) chord. This means that we've taken the basic Gm7 chord form and added a first-string C note. This notation can get a bit confusing, as you'll see in measure 18. The chord name Am7♭5(D) refers to the Am7 flat-five chord with a D melody note added. The top note of the chord is always the melody note.

Play the chord-melody version of "Avalon" very slowly at first, making sure that the melody can be heard above the accompaniment. You can do this by fingerpicking in a kind of plucking motion, with a flatpick sweeping across the strings and ending on the melody, or with your bare thumb.

Avalon

Music by Vincent Rose, lyrics by Al Jolson and B.G. DeSylva

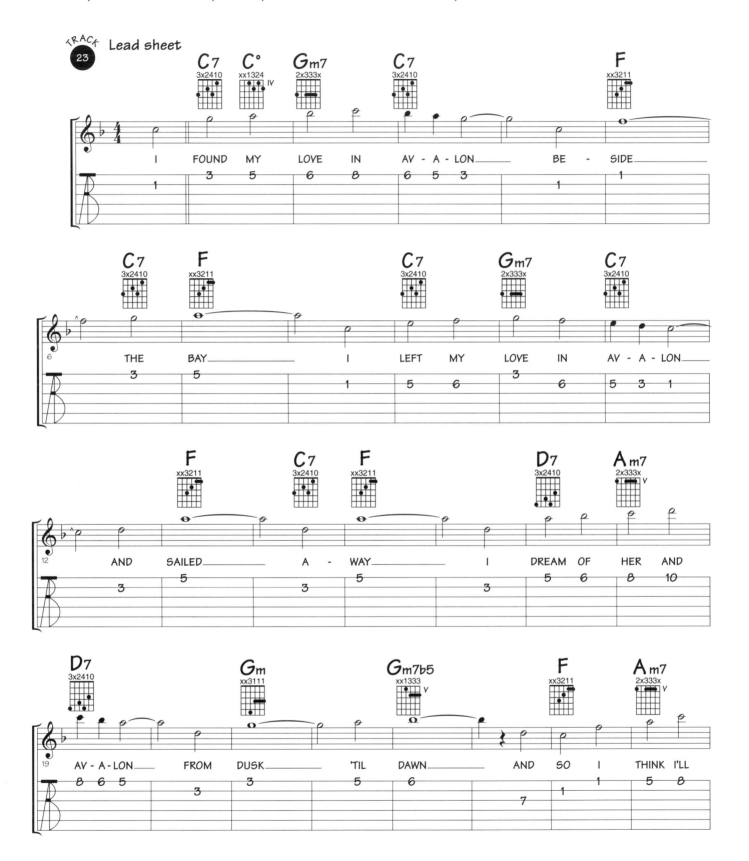

© 1920 Warner Bros., Inc. (ASCAP). All rights reserved. Used by permission. Warner Bros. Publishing U.S., Inc., Miami, FL 33014.

To arrange "Avalon," I started with the original sheet music (which listed the names of all the chords), transposed the melody up an octave, and added chords to the melody by using an inverted or up-the-neck version of the simple, first-position chord. In many cases (measures 3, 8, 9, and 10, for example) I left out the chord and played a single-string melody note for variety's sake. As you play these single notes, try to keep your fretting hand in the same basic shape in which it played the previous chord. For example, when playing the third-string C note in measure 8, keep your fretting hand in its F6 chord position. Try adding chords in the places where I left them out. As you do so, try not to switch hand positions too much; the idea, again, is to conserve hand motion. You could also go the other way and eliminate some of the chords I've included. It's all up to you.

Measures 31–34 illustrate a typical extended ending. As originally written, the song's last four bars have a ii–V–I passage, with one measure each of Gm7 (ii) and C7 (V) and two measures of F (I). The melody and chordal accompaniment in measures 31 and 32 of my arrangement are basically the same as in measures 29 and 30 of the original, but moved up one whole step. This changes the ii–V (Gm7–C7) to a iii–VI (Am7–D7). The original ii–V pattern from measures 29 and 30 shows up in measures 33 and 34 of my version, although I've substituted a C13 for the original C7, and the last two measures are a plain old F chord. This type of ending is called a iii–VI–ii–V.

It may take you weeks or months to master this arrangement of "Avalon." Once you feel comfortable with it as written, try a few of these variations: Substitute the F6 chord below for the Fmaj7 in measure 13. Substitute the C9 chord below for the C9 given on beats 3 and 4 in measure 3. Use the same form to play the D9 on beats 3 and 4 in measure 19.

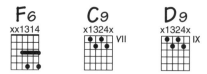

How do these forms affect the goal of minimum hand movement mentioned before? Can you change the chord forms so that adjacent chords in the passage are in the same general neck position? Try playing the Gm7 below as the first chord of measure 1, the Caug on beats 3 and 4 of measure 8, and the C13♭9 in measure 34.

Once you've tired of my chord-melody arrangement, it's time to work on your own. In order to arrange chord melodies for your favorite tunes, you need to choose a key and octave that will allow the melody to be played easily on the treble strings. On tunes with a wide range of low and high notes, you may have to move from octave to octave to find the smoothest transitions between chords. Again, try to stay in a given position on the neck as long as possible and avoid unnecessary motion in your fretting hand.

Finding the actual chords may be problematic, especially if you are a beginner. Consult a good guitar chord dictionary for inspiration and always remember to use your ears. It's also a good idea to write down your arrangements in a bound music notebook for future study. Most importantly, listen to the jazz guitar greats play chord melody and analyze their work.

Swing Soloing

David Hamburger

PART ONE

SWINGING A BLUES

As with so much American music, the blues is at the root of many styles of swing, so let's initiate our introduction to swing soloing by playing a C blues from a swing perspective. We'll begin by pulling out the root, third, fifth, and sixth of the major scale to form a basic unit for soloing: the major sixth arpeggio. Next, we'll look at how phrasing affects the sound of these arpeggios and how sequencing from chord to chord—playing a C arpeggio over a C chord, changing to an F arpeggio over an F chord, and so on—works to create the swing sound. We'll check out a few essential moves, such as chord-tone embellishment, and look at ideas for developing an improvisational vocabulary before wrapping things up with a 12-bar chorus of blues in C, swing style.

Have you ever tried playing a plain major scale in a solo? The poor major scale sounds so lame and exercise-like, yet it's full of good notes. Let's take the root, the third, and the fifth (the basic triad tones of a C major chord) and throw in the sixth to make things interesting. The result is called a C major sixth arpeggio.

The major sixth arpeggio has a vocabulary of pet licks and idiomatic moves that everyone uses.

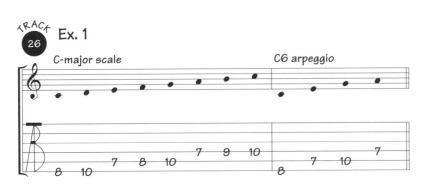

OK, it still sounds a little lame, it's true. That's because it's still just an arpeggio lying helpless on the page. It's just a skeleton of an idea, not a musical message. Your own skeleton can't get up and dance all by itself; it needs muscles to pull it around, flesh to hold things together, and your brain up on top to listen to the music and tell the feet, legs, and arms where to go and when.

Example 2 is a dancing lesson for your arpeggio. Slide into every major third with a grace note from a half step below. Rhythmically, this two-octave–plus extravaganza is phrased so that those slides into the major third are always on a strong downbeat—the first or third beat of a measure.

Introduction

Now, wouldn't it be great to be able to play this phrase elsewhere, say in F and G? No, we're *not* just going to move it up five frets; that's too easy, and besides, it doesn't look cool. (There are two ways to look cool on the guitar. One is to play the same thing over and over, but to play it everywhere you conceivably can on the fretboard. The other, more subtle way to be cool is to play all different kinds of things in one position, without moving at all.)

Example 3 shows the basic F-major scale, followed by the root, third, fifth, and sixth in F, and finally the full-flavor dance-lesson F major sixth arpeggio, all played in the seventh position.

Let's take G through the same steps.

Once you can play all the arpeggios comfortably, practice them further by going through a C blues, changing arpeggios whenever the chord changes.

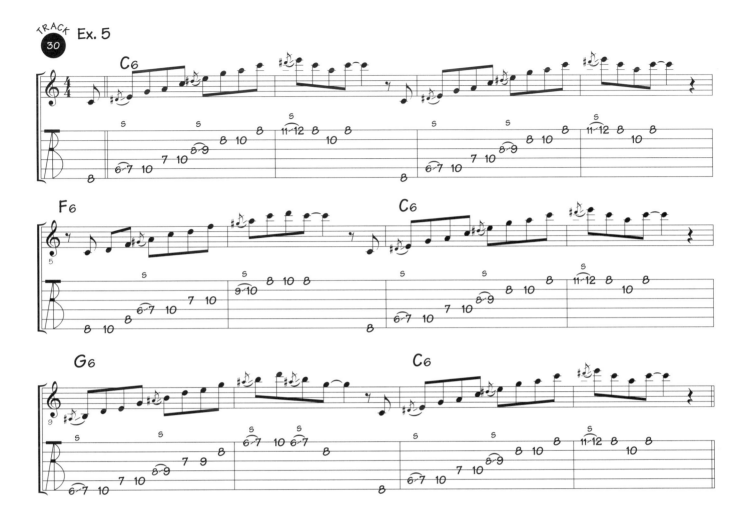

When learning a new style and beginning to improvise with new fingerings, it's not uncommon to fall into one of two traps. The first trap comes from learning the scales or arpeggios as whole units and being unable to break them apart. What results are solos that consist of mechanically running up and down a series of lumbering two-octave fingerings, which ends up sounding more like an exercise than an improvisation. The second trap is to break up the various scales and/or arpeggios so finely that the resulting solos sound completely random, a grab bag of available notes that have no connection to one another whatsoever. Either way, confusion results. These are the right scales, the right notes—why doesn't it sound right?

Part of the answer is that learning any style of improvising has to do with vocabulary. Just like the minor pentatonic scale in Chicago blues, or the open-G position in bluegrass, the major sixth arpeggio has a vocabulary of pet licks and idiomatic moves that everyone uses to play swing. Learning some of those licks and moves can serve as a middle path between the twin traps described above. Each measure in Example 6 consists of four eighth notes that come directly from the C major sixth arpeggio. Each group hangs together as a bit of a lick, a typical swing-style move or building block. Note the numerous slides into the third.

TRACK
31 **Ex. 6**

Now comes the fun part. Learn each of these four-note units and then try stringing them together. You can be systematic about it—matching the first one with each of the following ones, matching the second with every other one, etc., and then picking the best ones—or you can just spin around randomly. If you make random connections now, you are connecting things that already work; the four-note units are your stylistic safety net. Of course, you shouldn't get too hooked on the combinations you come up with, or you'll be back to playing prepared stuff that you can't break apart and reshape in the heat of the moment.

The licks in Example 7 were created by combining the various units from Example 6.

TRACK
32 **Ex. 7**

Transposing these licks to G and F presents the question of whether it's better to go up or down in register. Some licks will go up easily, like the one from Example 7, which I've shown transposed to F (Example 8) and to G (Example 9).

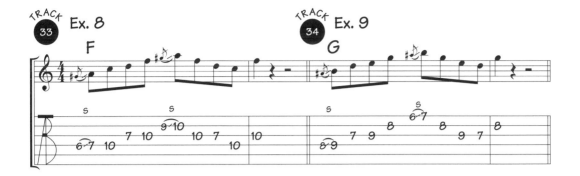

Others will need to be taken down in order to transpose all the notes correctly and still stay in position (and thus look cool). Check out the second lick from Example 7 transposed down to F (Example 10) and to G (Example 11).

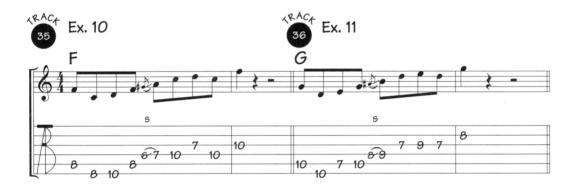

NEIGHBOR TONES

One of the easiest ways to embellish or add to an arpeggio is to add in *neighbor tones.* Generally speaking, neighbor tones are notes a major or minor second above or below any note that belongs in a particular scale or arpeggio. More specifically, a *chromatic neighbor tone* is one half step (a minor second) above or below a given scale or arpeggio note. A *lower chromatic neighbor tone* is the note a half step *below* a given scale or chord tone. So, for example, the lower chromatic neighbor tone of C is B♮. The lower chromatic neighbor tone of G is F♯. Example 12 illustrates the C, F, and G major sixth arpeggios, with each note of each arpeggio preceded by its lower chromatic neighbor tone.

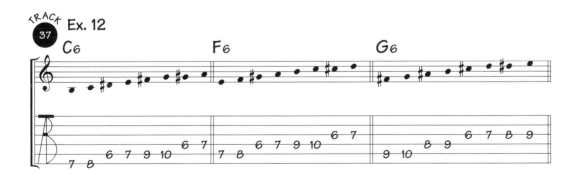

Using neighbor tones is very convenient, because you get to add in all these interest-ing-sounding notes without having to really remember much more than the original arpeggio notes. Example 13 is a good exercise for working these notes into a full-sized fingering of the arpeggio. It's shown in C; try working it out in F and G, beginning with the fingerings shown in Examples 3 and 4.

Of course, you'll need some sound bites you can move around with this approach, too. Example 14 will give you a few ideas to get you rolling. See if you can transpose the licks in Example 14 to F and G, and then take Example 15 out for a spin. It's a 12-bar blues in C that uses major sixth arpeggios, slides into the third, changes arpeggios when the chords change, and uses chromatic lower neighbor tones with each arpeggio.

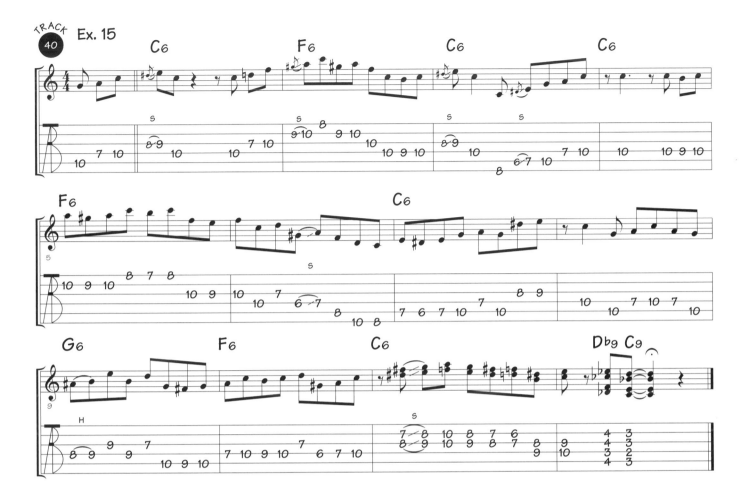

PART TWO

Some of the basic concepts of swing-style soloing include using major sixth arpeggios, changing arpeggios when the chord changes, using lower chromatic neighbor tones, and sliding into the major third. Let's take each of these ideas a little further, thickening the stew with some mixolydian scales, dominant seventh and minor sixth arpeggios, and chromatic passing tones. We'll also check out how different kinds of melodic sequencing can be part of developing an improvised solo.

Introduction   TRACK 41

A LA MODE

The mixolydian mode is particularly useful for swing and blues soloing. *Mode* is simply another word for scale, and there are many ways of deriving and describing the various modes. For our immediate purposes, you can think of the mixolydian scale as a major scale with the seventh flatted or lowered a half step. So a C mixolydian scale is like a C major scale with a B♭ replacing the B.

TRACK 42 **Ex. 1**

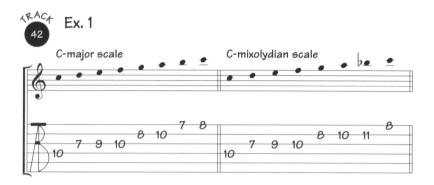

Now we can create an arpeggio by pulling out notes from this scale, just as we created the C major sixth arpeggio by pulling out notes from the C major scale. If we take the root, third, fifth, and seventh notes of this C mixolydian scale, we get something called a C dominant seventh arpeggio.

TRACK 43 **Ex. 2**

C7 arpeggio

This sound is also referred to as a C7—or C mixolydian—arpeggio. We can finger this arpeggio in almost the same way as the C major sixth arpeggio; we just take the C major sixth arpeggio and change the sixths (A's), to flatted sevenths (B♭'s), as shown in Example 3.

TRACK 44 **Ex. 3**

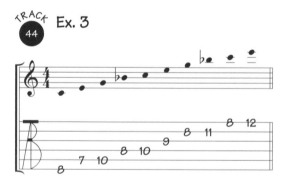

Example 4 shows the same kind of phrasing exercise for C7 that we used for the C6 in part one (Example 2, page 34).

If you pick apart the notes of a C7 chord, you'll notice that it's a C major triad with a B♭ added:

In other words, the notes of a C7 chord are those of a C7 arpeggio, which is why this arpeggio is so useful to us—we can play a C7 arpeggio over a C7 chord, switch to an F7 arpeggio over an F7 chord, and then play a G7 arpeggio over a G7 chord. In Example 5 you'll find the mixolydian scale, seventh arpeggio, two-octave fingering, and phrasing exercise in F, and in Example 6 in G. You can get a lot of mileage out of just these three scales.

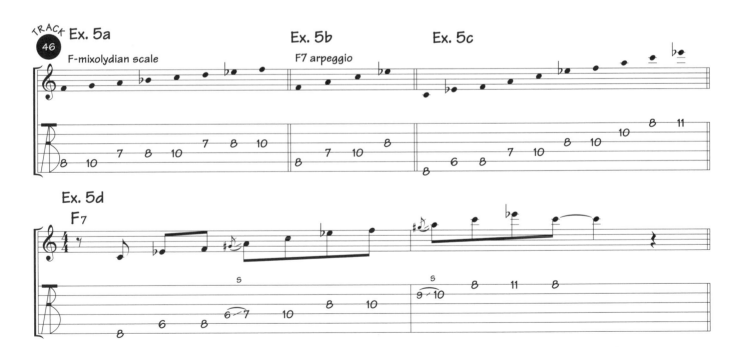

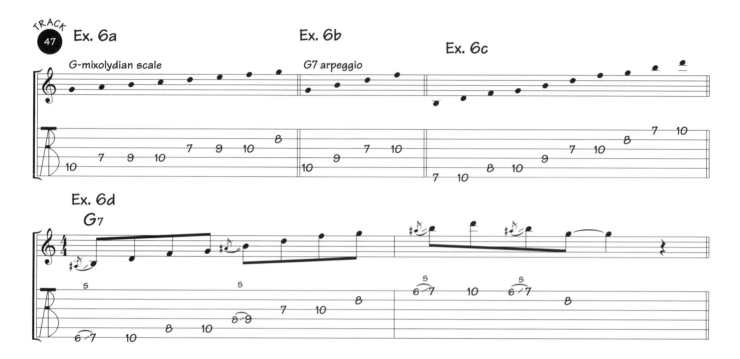

Example 7 is a 12-bar solo on a C blues using only notes of the C7 arpeggio on the C chord, notes of the F7 arpeggio on the F chord, and notes of the G7 arpeggio on the G chord.

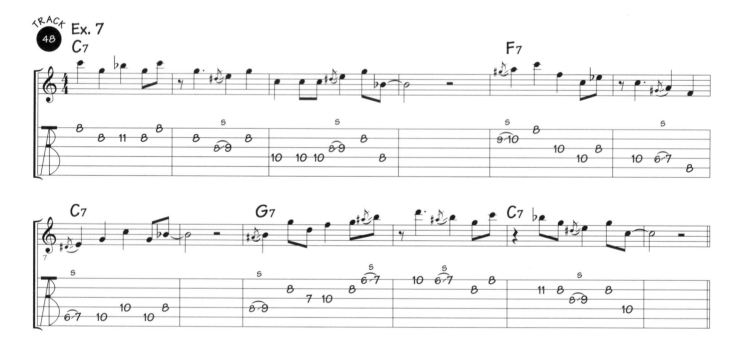

Being able to match modes to chords correctly and on the spot is an essential skill, but it's just the first piece of the puzzle. Let's look now at some more ideas about phrasing, melodic development, and chromaticism, which are just a few of the tools that can help you bring these basic arpeggios to life.

PHRASING

By simply paying attention to the phrasing of an arpeggio, you can make it sound more musical—by sliding into the major third, for instance, and by timing it so that the thirds all fall on strong beats. We can develop this idea further by focusing on creating phrases with the mixolydian arpeggio that begin with three eighth notes leading into the downbeat (on the *and* of 3), or else just after the downbeat (on the *and* of 1). Both of these are typical of swing phrasing. For instance, both phrases in Example 8 lead into the downbeat, using a C mixolydian scale.

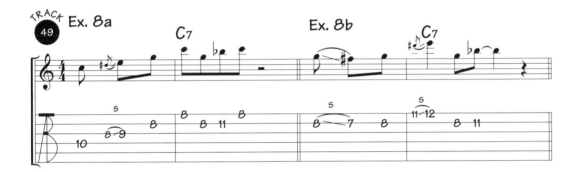

In contrast, the two phrases in Example 9 each begin just after the downbeat.

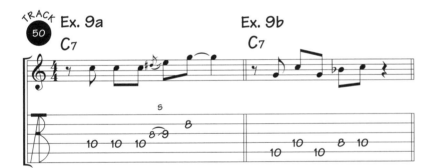

All of these examples use nothing but arpeggio notes (except for the lower chromatic neighbor tone—the F♯—in Example 8b), but their phrasing makes them sound more like music and less like exercises.

Sequencing is common in all forms of music, but it can be an especially useful tool for the swing improviser. Sequencing generally refers to the repetition of an idea. For example, you could play Example 8a and then transpose it to F, keeping the phrasing and choice of notes intact, as shown in Example 10.

Someone smart once pointed out, "You can't have a theme and variations without a theme." In other words, a solo that aspires to be all variation will leave everyone dissatisfied in the end. Of course, one of the great skills of improvising is knowing how much to repeat and when to move on. Bill Barron, the tenor saxophonist, composer, and teacher, suggested that three times was really the limit for a repetition—the same note, the same phrase, the same lick—and then you'd better make something else of it. In Example 11, we begin with a phrase over C7, sequence it over the F7 chord, repeat the original phrase back on C7, and then *extend it* into something new in measure 4.

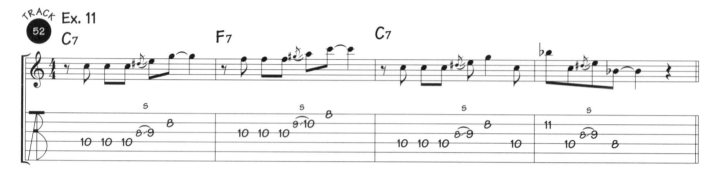

COMMON TONES

Another form of sequencing is sometimes called *common tone sequencing.* I got this idea from jazz guitarist Peter Einhorn, and it really opened things up for me. When the chord changes, instead of transposing your phrase note for note to the arpeggio that matches the new chord, you repeat the phrase right where you are, changing only those notes that you have to change to fit the new chord. In other words, you keep all the notes that the two chords have in common.

For example, let's go back to the major sixth arpeggios we used in part one—the root, third, fifth, and sixth of a major scale, or C, E, G, and A in the key of C. All you have to do to make this arpeggio fit over an F7 chord is change all the E♮ notes to E♭. You could think of the resulting arpeggio as a C minor sixth arpeggio (C, E♭, G, A; or root, minor third, fifth, sixth) or as part of an F7 arpeggio with the second (or ninth) note of the F mixolydian scale thrown in. C, E♭, G, and A are the fifth, flatted seventh, ninth, and third of the F mixolydian scale. Example 12 shows the C major sixth and C minor sixth arpeggios side by side.

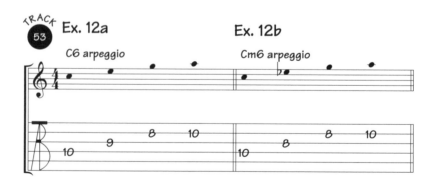

To execute a common tone sequence, begin with an ordinary C major sixth lick over the C chord, switch to the C minor sixth arpeggio, and then repeat the lick over the F chord using E♭ instead of E, as in Example 13.

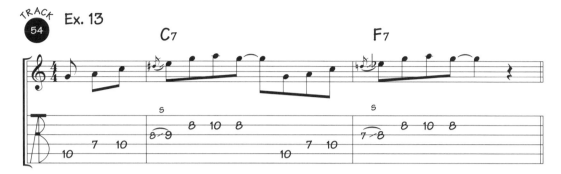

PASSING TONES

We can also make use of chromatic *passing* tones—notes that fall in between two notes a whole step apart. In Example 14, B♮ is the chromatic passing tone between the root and the ♭7 of the C7 arpeggio. In Example 15, A♭ is the chromatic passing tone between the sixth and the fifth of the C major sixth arpeggio.

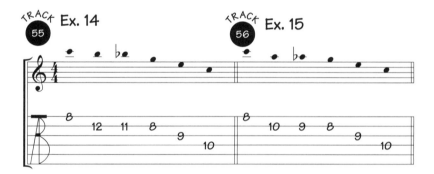

Chromatic passing tones can be used to smooth out descending lines, punctuate the end of a phrase, or give the whole phrase a kind of twisted quality, as if the melody is turning back on itself. Examples 16 and 17 combine elements of both the C major sixth and C7 arpeggios. Example 16 begins with the major sixth sound before going into a chromatic passing tone from the root to the ♭7 of the C7 arpeggio in the second half of the first measure. This same move occurs in the first half of the second measure of Example 17, after a whole measure in the major sixth arpeggio.

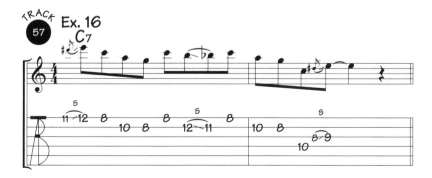

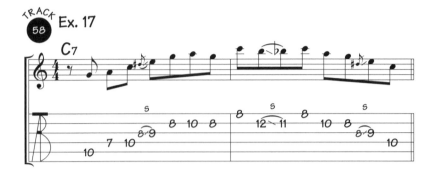

Example 18 is in F. In the first full measure, there is a chromatic move from the sixth to the fifth (D, D♭, C on the high string) followed by a descent from the root to the ♭7 that concludes in the next bar (F, E, E♭ on the G string) before jumping up to repeat the sixth-to-fifth chromatic move.

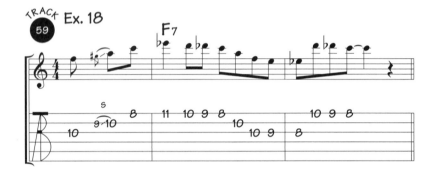

Example 19, in G, is just the opposite. The first full measure begins with a root-to-♭7 chromatic move (G, G♭, F on the second and third strings) before going to a sixth-to-fifth chromatic move (E, E♭, D on the G string). It ends with a repeat of the root-to-♭7 move an octave down (on the A string).

PUTTING IT ALL TOGETHER

Let's see what happens when we put some of these ideas together. Example 20 is a chorus of swinging blues in C to sink your fingers into. It kicks off with a C major sixth phrase that leads into the downbeat. This is answered with a C7 lick that also passes chromatically from the sixth to the fifth. The opening phrase is then repeated going into the third bar, and it's answered going into the fourth bar with a new major sixth phrase. This last

C major sixth phrase is repeated via a common tone sequence in measure 5, using the C minor sixth arpeggio and then added to in measure 6. In measure 7, this newest phrase is sequenced *back into* a major sixth phrase and ended with a chromatic move from root down to ♭7. Measures 9 and 10 show how the chromatic G lick from Example 19 can fit into an actual playing situation with a slightly different three-note pickup into the downbeat. It is followed by a three-note pickup back into the land of C major sixth, and the example ends with a couple of funky 13th chords, which, as my high school guitar teacher pointed out, are a good thing to know when you're going downtown to try out those fat jazz guitars.

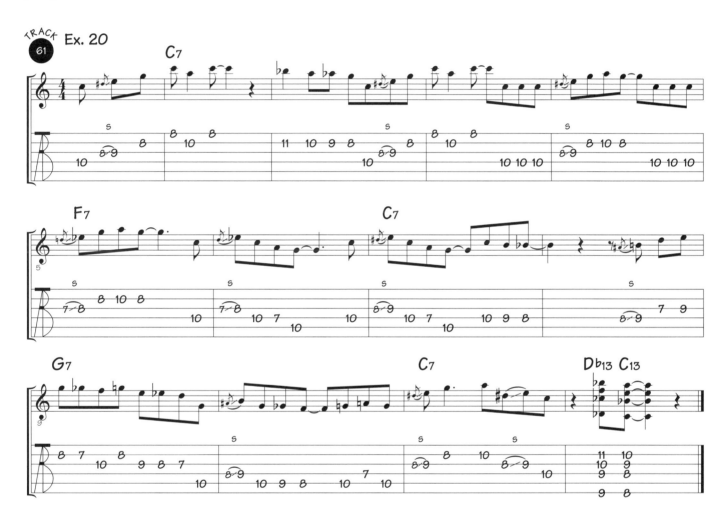

an introduction to early jazz

Tony Marcus

Pioneering jazzer Eddie Lang.

The use of the guitar goes back to the very beginnings of jazz. When legendary cornetist Buddy Bolden played in New Orleans before the turn of the 20th century, the chordal instrument of choice was guitar. Jeff Mumford (1870–1937) and Charlie Galloway (1865–1914) are two of the guitarists who accompanied Bolden in bands that were making the first steps in the music that became jazz. Interestingly enough, these bands (like many New Orleans groups) utilized string bass rather than tuba. This combination of guitar and bass would not become the standard in dance and jazz bands throughout the country until the early 1930s.

During the '20s, the jazz craze that had begun with the Original Dixieland Jazz Band's incursion into New York society in 1917 mostly relied on the banjo/tuba rhythm section. A few guitarists, such as Lonnie Johnson (who recorded with Duke Ellington), Bernard Addison (who worked with Louis Armstrong and Jelly Roll Morton, among others), and the almost unknown Ed "Snoozer" Quinn, were working in a jazz context, but when it came to plectrum instruments, the Jazz Age of the '20s was an age of tenor banjos.

EDDIE LANG ARRIVES

Eddie Lang, born Salvatore Massaro in Philadelphia in 1902, did the most to bring the guitar into dance and jazz bands. Originally a violinist (as was his longtime musical partner, Joe Venuti), Lang started experimenting with both banjo and guitar at an early age. While a four-string banjo player was de rigueur for dance bands in the '20s, guitar was seldom used. This situation was due in part to the recording technology of the day. The microphone wasn't invented until 1925, and on acoustic recordings (where the musicians had to play into a huge horn), the guitar's sound was very difficult to capture on wax, particularly in the context of brass and woodwinds. Lang worked early on with Chick Granese's Trio, Charlie Kerr's Band (1920–1923), and the Scranton Sirens (1924). In most of these bands, Lang doubled on banjo and guitar—and occasionally played violin.

In 1924 Lang joined the Mound City Blue Blowers, a novelty group that featured the comb-and-tissue-paper antics of Red McKenzie. It was with this group that Lang made his first record. By 1929 he was working with the Paul Whiteman Orchestra. Band leaders such as Whiteman placed Lang very close to the new miracle microphone, and he played amazing arpeggios and bass lines to hold the sound of the band together. Lang's prodigious ear enabled him to play arrangements without ever looking at a page of music. Supposedly he had the Whiteman Orchestra's complete book of arrangements on the back of a business card. He found himself so much in demand that he would often work three or four jobs in a single day.

Eddie Lang with the Mound City Blue Blowers.

VENUTI AND LANG

Lang and violinist Joe Venuti recorded together in small groups that allowed them time to stretch out a bit and in larger orchestras where they might be afforded a few measures of solo time. Their inventive duets, often based on the chord changes of other tunes, were like nothing heard before: indisputable hot jazz played on instruments that were almost unknown in this context. These recordings inspired Django Reinhardt and Stéphane Grappelli to explore Gypsy jazz in Paris a few years later. Venuti's fiery inventions are off-set perfectly by Lang's chordal support and runs. The resulting performances are an intriguing blend of ragtime, Italian music, blues phrases, and the harmonic vocabulary of 1920s jazz.

LONNIE JOHNSON AND BLUES DUETS

Alonzo "Lonnie" Johnson was born in New Orleans at the turn of the century. Like Lang, he was a violinist as a child (as well as a pianist). He had already toured as far afield as Scotland when, in 1925, he won a contest organized by the Okeh Record Co. This led to Johnson's career as a blues guitarist. He made many records in the country blues vein in the '20s that show his mastery of the idiom. Possessed of a sweet voice and a flashy rhythmic guitar style, he continued his career (which included an R&B hit with the song

SELECTED DISCOGRAPHY

Lonnie Johnson, *Steppin' on the Blues,* Sony/Legacy 46221. A collection that includes a few duets with Eddie Lang.

Eddie Lang, *Jazz Guitar Virtuoso,* Yazoo 1059. Mostly duets with Johnson and a number of piano players. Yazoo, distributed by Shanachie, 13 Laight St., Sixth Floor, New York, NY 10013; (212) 334-0284; hanach@idt.net; www.shanachie.com.

Eddie Lang, *The Quintessential Eddie Lang: 1925–1932,* Timeless 043. A varied collection that includes duets with Joe Venuti and Johnson and tracks with Frankie Trumbauer, Louis Armstrong, Bessie Smith, Bing Crosby, and many others. Timeless, PO Box 201, 6700 AE Wageningen, Holland; fax (31) 0317-421548; www.wwmusic.com/timeless.

Eddie Lang, *A Handful of Riffs,* ASV 5061. Duets with Johnson and piano players and a number of tracks by Lang and his Orchestra. ASV, distributed by Pinnacle, Unit 2, Orpington Trading Estate, Sevenoaks Wy., Orpington, Kent BR5 3SR, England.

Charlie Palloy, *Vocals and Guitar,* The Old Masters 118. The Old Masters, PO Box 25358, San Mateo, CA 94401; (650) 520-4425.

Various artists, *Pioneers of the Jazz Guitar,* Yazoo 1057. An indispensable collection that includes Lang, Johnson, Carl Kress, Dick McDonough, Nick Lucas, and others.

"Tomorrow Night" in 1948) off and on until his death in 1970. Johnson was also featured with the Duke Ellington Orchestra on a number of sides in the late '20s. These recordings show him fitting well with a large group, although he didn't always sound as comfortable as he did playing solo. Johnson and Lang also recorded a historic group of blues-based guitar duets (almost entirely with Lang playing rhythm for Johnson's solos). For these sides, Lang used the pseudonym Blind Willie Dunn. It was unheard of at that time for black and white musicians to record together, and Okeh Records released these sides in its "race" category.

LANG'S GUITAR

The earliest picture of Eddie Lang with a guitar shows him playing a fairly large flattop, likely a Stella or a Galiano. He soon moved on to an archtop Gibson L-4 (the early oval-

Bing Crosby with Eddie Lang.

hole variety). Jazz guitar legend George Van Eps recalled that in 1925 Lang allowed the 12-year-old Van Eps to borrow this guitar overnight, thus cementing the direction of his musical career. Shortly thereafter, Lang availed himself of one of the new Gibson L-5 guitars. These pioneering instruments were the first production guitars with f-holes as well as carved tops and backs. This "cello" design was perfect for the new style of playing that Lang developed. He strung his guitar with what would seem to a modern player to be extremely heavy strings (.015, .018, .030, .036, .048, .075) so as to achieve maximum volume. Gibson apparently supplied Lang with a new L-5 every two years. It could be that the heavy strings were taking their toll on the guitars' tops or necks.

ACCOMPANYING BING CROSBY

In 1930, the Whiteman Orchestra (which was based in New York City) went to California for the filming of *King Of Jazz,* a revue-style feature that was centered around the band (there is a brief scene of Lang and Venuti playing a duet). While there, Bing Crosby (who was singing with Whiteman in the vocal trio the Rhythm Boys) embarked on the start of his groundbreaking solo career. He brought along the one musician he thought indispensable: Eddie Lang. For this job, Lang earned the then unheard-of sum of $1,000 per week. For the rest of his life, Lang was Crosby's accompanist, though this didn't preclude his playing in many other combinations. (That this grouping was successful is proven by the recordings of the mysterious Charlie Palloy. Recording for the bargain Crown label in 1932–33, Palloy's singing and guitar playing were a credible imitation of both Crosby and Lang.) Lang made screen appearances backing Crosby, most notably in *The Big Broadcast.* In 1933 Lang, who had been plagued by health problems but was shy of doctors, went into the hospital for a tonsillectomy. Though the surgery was routine, Lang developed an embolism on the operating table and died without regaining consciousness. He was 30 years old.

Eddie Lang-Style Swing Blues

Tony Marcus

Unlike pioneering New York guitarists Roy Smeck and Nick Lucas, the sensibility that Eddie Lang brought to his music was not that of the vaudeville stage. With Smeck particularly, the remains of the ragtime craze were mingled with whatever novelty effects might combine for the greatest audience response. The road Lang followed was to try to discover a way for the humble guitar to take its place alongside the rest of the band—to find the voice of the instrument for the 20th century. He synthesized the traditional Italian music that he had heard as a child with the Jazz Age rhythms of the '20s and came up with something entirely new. From a modern perspective, some critics have attacked Lang's rhythm playing as being stiff. He certainly didn't have the rhythmic fluidity of Freddie Green (see "Freddie Green's Rhythm Style," page 55), but Lang predated Green by eons in terms of jazz history.

The style he created was amazingly varied. In a duo or small group setting, Lang would create a filigree around his chords. His bag of tricks included bass lines (often in eighth-note triplets), accented single-note upbeats followed by chords on the downbeat, harmonics, and bluesy fills.

Perhaps the most interesting thing about Lang's innovations, however, is how much they came and went with him. At the time of his death (in 1933), the rhythmic feel of the music was undergoing a basic change. A 2/4 rhythm, with the tuba playing two notes per measure, had until then been the norm for both dance bands and "hot jazz" combos, but it was swiftly becoming old-fashioned. The new sound, which would form the basis of the swing era, was a loping 4/4 rhythm. The string bass usurped the tuba's place in bands and tended to play four quarter notes per measure. The banjo had largely been discarded when bandleaders heard Lang's new sound, but it would have been ungainly in the swing context anyway. Guitarists in the big bands of the '30s mostly spent their time plugging away playing a steady four chords per measure. Teddy Bunn (of the Spirits of Rhythm and other small groups) and a few others who continued to play single-string solos were the exceptions. Almost all the orchestra guitarists either stuck strictly to rhythm playing or soloed in the banjo-derived chordal style (see "Beginning Chord Melody," page 27). If they had learned Eddie Lang's musical language, they no longer had a forum for it. When the guitar returned to the jazz forefront in a soloing context, it would be plugged in, and everything would be different.

In the blues chorus written out here, I've imagined Lang double-tracked, playing accompaniment to himself. Notice the rolled arpeggios rather than straight four-to-the-bar chords in the first two measures of the rhythm guitar part. The bass figure, starting with the triplet in measure 4, is also very typical of his style. Note the way that the A7 chord in measures 5 and 6 is voiced in different inversions up the neck. The solo is very simple and straightforward but does utilize a number of effects Lang was fond of. There is not an overwhelming amount of syncopation, but it doesn't have the stiff feel of Nick Lucas' solo records. Note the use of harmonics in measures 3, 4, and 12. The triplet eighth-note figures in measure 3 are characteristic as well. There is also a string bend in measure 6, a device that Lang might have been the first white guitarist to employ.

Lang synthesized the traditional Italian music that he had heard as a child with Jazz Age rhythms.

Introduction

Been There, Dunn That Blues

Music by Tony Marcus

an introduction to big-band swing

Michael Simmons

Although the guitar was present at the birth of jazz—an 1895 photograph of legendary cornet player Buddy Bolden shows one of his fellow musicians holding a parlor-size guitar—most early jazz bands chose to use the much louder banjo instead. The Gibson L-5 archtop, introduced in 1924, was the first guitar with enough volume to be heard over the drums and horns of a typical jazz band.

This new archtop style of guitar had a smoother tone than the banjo, as well as an expanded harmonic range. Gibson's L-5, along with the guitars of its competitors Epiphone and D'Angelico, proved to be so popular that by the early '30s if a band was still using a banjo, it was considered to be old-fashioned. Banjo players had to learn to play the new instrument or lose their jobs. Fred Guy, who joined Duke Ellington's band in 1925 as a banjoist, managed to resist the change longer than most, but by the end of the decade he too was a guitarist. When Ellington's band was touring England in 1933, critic Spike Hughes said he preferred it when Guy "played guitar, but that was principally because he wasn't playing banjo."

By 1935 swing was the dominant style of jazz, and the king of swing was Benny Goodman. Goodman was a brilliant musician but a difficult man to work for. Perhaps that is why he attracted the best musicians to play for him and almost as quickly drove them away. Other bands took advantage of Goodman's high turnover, and by 1940 there probably wasn't a band in the country that didn't have at least one Goodman alumnus in its roster. One of the first guitarists to work with Goodman was Dick McDonough, whose L-5 can be heard on such early classics as "Ain'tcha Glad" and "I've Got a Right to Sing the Blues." McDonough also recorded a series of duets with Carl Kress that have come to be regarded as jazz guitar classics.

McDonough's replacement was George Van Eps, who later went on to pioneer the seven-string guitar. He was one of the first big-band guitarists to play an instrument by Epiphone, the company that became Gibson's main rival in the '30s. Van Eps' tenure with Goodman was brief, but during his year with the band he recorded one of his first solos on "Love Me or Leave Me." In his book *The History of Guitar in Jazz,* Norman Mongan says that Van Eps was often at odds with Goodman because of his habit of "taking sophisticated harmonic liberties with the standard chord parts." In 1935 Van Eps missed a gig because of another commitment, and Goodman hired a replacement, Allan Reuss. Reuss managed to stay with Goodman until 1938, and his solid playing on a blond L-5 anchored the rhythm section. He left after an argument with Goodman and later joined Paul Whiteman's band.

In 1939 Charlie Christian joined the Goodman band. Just as the introduction of the L-5 hastened the end of the banjo in jazz, Christian's use of the amplified Gibson ES-150

Basie guitarist Freddie Green.

SELECTED DISCOGRAPHY

FREDDIE GREEN

Count Basie, *The Complete Decca Recordings,* GRP/Decca 611. A three-CD set with many big-band classics and several quartet tracks (with Basie on piano).

Count Basie and His Orchestra, *April in Paris,* Verve 521-402. A rerelease of the classic 1956 LP, with alternate takes. Includes the Green composition "Corner Pocket."

Rhythm Willie, Concord Jazz 6010. Quartet with Green backing up Herb Ellis on electric lead. Concord Jazz, PO Box 845, Concord, CA 94522; (510) 682-6770; www.aent.com/concord.

Green: keeping the pulse.

SELECTED DISCOGRAPHY

ALLAN REUSS

Benny Goodman Plays Fletcher Henderson, Hep 1038. Reuss on rhythm guitar, except for four cuts where George Van Eps takes over. Hep, PO Box 50, Edinburgh EH7 5DA, Scotland; fax (44) 131-556-8145; heprecords@expressmedia.co.uk; www.expressmedia.co.uk/heprecords/.

Lionel Hampton and His Orchestra, 1937–1938, Classics 524. Classics/Qualiton, 24-02 40th Ave., Long Island City, NY 11101; (718) 937-8515.

GEORGE VAN EPS

Red Norvo, *Dance of the Octopus,* Hep 1044. Van Eps plays rhythm on some cuts.

Adrian Rollini, *Swing Low,* Affinity 1030. Van Eps on five cuts, with solos on two. Affinity, 156–166 Ilderton Rd., London SE15 1NT, England.

meant that the acoustic guitar's role in jazz would soon be over. By the early '40s more and more players were taking up the new style of guitar, and by the end of the decade swing music was no longer the dominant form of jazz. Bebop, a style created in after-hours jam sessions in small clubs like Minton's by musicians like Christian, Dizzy Gillespie, and Thelonious Monk was now the direction in which jazz was headed.

In 1937, the year before Charlie Christian revolutionized jazz guitar, Freddie Green took over the guitar chair from Claude Williams in the Count Basie band. In his 50 years with the band, Green's playing has come to define swing guitar. Unlike the Goodman band, which recycled players at an alarming rate, the Basie orchestra tended to hold on to musicians. This meant that Green—along with bassist Walter Page, drummer Jo Jones, and Basie on piano—had the time to work out the subtleties of harmony and rhythm that made them the strongest rhythm section in jazz.

Green didn't start out as a rhythm man. He was a single-string player when he joined Basie. In Mongan's *The History of Guitar in Jazz,* he is quoted as saying, "I experimented with a couple of single-string things with Basie in 1937. About half a chorus. But there was so much going on, that the only thing to do was play rhythm." Because of his long association with Page and Jones, Green was able to develop a style that stripped rhythm guitar to the basics. He rarely played more than three or four strings in a chord, but his steady four-chords-to-the-bar style supplied a rich harmonic base for the soloists while maintaining the strong pulse that held the rhythm section together.

Green's main guitar was a Stromberg Master 400, although in his later years he played a Gretsch. He played with heavy strings and high action. It is a testament to his physical strength that although he never played amplified, you could always hear him chunking away in the background of even the loudest tunes.

In the early '50s, bop replaced swing on the turntables of jazz fans, and promoters discovered that smaller (and cheaper) rock 'n' roll and R&B combos could still bring in dancers. The big bands began to break up, and many of the musicians retreated to New York and Los Angeles to find new careers as session players on records, television, and radio.

Today, although the era of the big band is definitely behind us, there are a number of guitarists working in the swing idiom. Players like Marty Grosz, Howard Alden, John Pizzarelli, and Tony Marcus are keeping the flame alive.

Freddie Green's Rhythm Style

John Lehmann-Haupt

JAY BERLINER

"In terms of rhythm guitar, Freddie Green stands above everyone else," said Jay Berliner. "He really made the sound of the Basie band, along with Basie's little right-hand fills on the piano. He was the foundation."

Berliner, one of three New York–based guitarists who shared their insights with me, has been at the very top of the New York studio scene for 35 years. He's played nearly 13,000 dates, recording with everyone from Frank Sinatra to Van Morrison, and his commanding chops, platinum ear, and wide stylistic range have enabled him to survive the onslaught of synthesizers and digital sampling with aplomb. Millions have also heard him on Garrison Keillor's American Radio Company and Prairie Home Companion shows.

Berliner spelled out the essentials. "It's the voicings, it's the approach, and it's the feel," he said. "Take a blues; most people play [*he strummed through a few standard-issue barre chords*]. You use that in the context of a big band or an orchestra, and the guitar's going to disappear. It's mud. The trick is to basically play three-note chords, with wide voicings," he said. "It makes a tremendous difference." He played the following four-chord progression, and the definition was unmistakable.

Three rhythm wizards share their secrets.

Introduction

"It also makes sense from the standpoint of physics that there should be space between the notes," he went on. "If you look at the way overtones work, the lower notes are farther apart, and the higher up you go the closer together they get. Each note sounds as part of a distinct line. You don't just jump from chord to chord," said Berliner. "It's voice leading. Often you don't play the root [usually sounded by the bass]. For example, here's a C7:

"There's no C. And if you just play a plain major chord, you usually make it a six chord [*see end of four-chord example, above*]. That's another part of the style."

Right-hand attack is critical, too. "With the pick, I'm looking for that middle string," Berliner continued. "Freddie Green would really just brush the other notes." Berliner played through another progression, this time nailing the central note, the outer two slightly damped. It was a revelation; I suddenly *got* the Freddie Green sound—up close, a brash honk of a line in an envelope at once harmonic and percussive, with pick sound and string slap adding to the mix. "It sounds simple, but it took years to really get it perfected," he commented.

And then there's rhythm. "Freddie Green's time was incredibly accurate and good," said Berliner. "It's about finding the pocket of various styles and tempos, or adjusting to certain drummers or rhythm sections. Sometimes you play a little behind the beat— not consciously, but you feel it just a little bit behind. Or if you're playing with someone like Oscar Peterson, you actually move up on top of the beat."

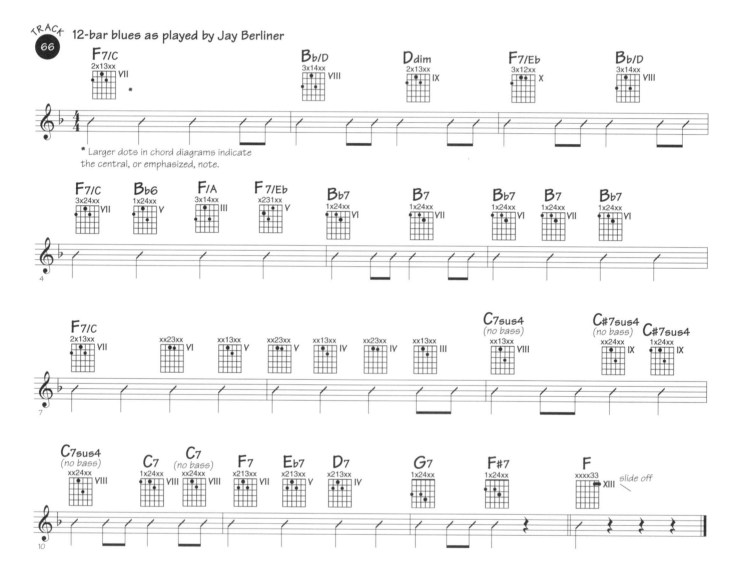

WAYNE WRIGHT

Wayne Wright is a guitarist who's played a great deal of rhythm in his career. He's backed up Benny Goodman, Gerry Mulligan, and Peggy Lee, to name a few, and he's also the man who coaxed Les Paul out of retirement, accompanying the Waukesha Wizard acoustically for the first six years of his legendary Monday-night engagement at Fat Tuesday's in New York City.

Wright cut his jazz teeth jamming with an impressive roster of older players in his native Detroit, among them pianist Tommy Flanagan, trumpeter Donald Byrd, and bass player Paul Chambers. His mentor in rhythm was none other than master drummer Elvin Jones.

"I had terrible time when I was a kid," said Wright, "and one day Elvin Jones said to me, 'Play rhythm, man! Have you ever heard of Freddie Green?'"

As he spoke, Wright began chunking through some improvised changes, snaking through some neat half-step substitutions and chromatic modulations—again, three-note voicings with clearly discernible lines. "Essentially what's going on is that interval of the tenth," he said, referring to the distance between the outer notes. "In the structure of the chord, there's the melody note, the bass note, and the one in between. I don't treat these as chords; I treat them as voices—all three."

Wright elaborated on the guitar's function in a group. "The first thing I do is lock in on the drums," he said, "whether we're right or wrong. Elvin Jones told me, 'If you're listening to me and I'm listening to you and we're wrong together, what's stronger than that?' The rhythm guitar is the catalyst between the impact of the drums and the tonality of the bass. This is the glue that keeps these guys together."

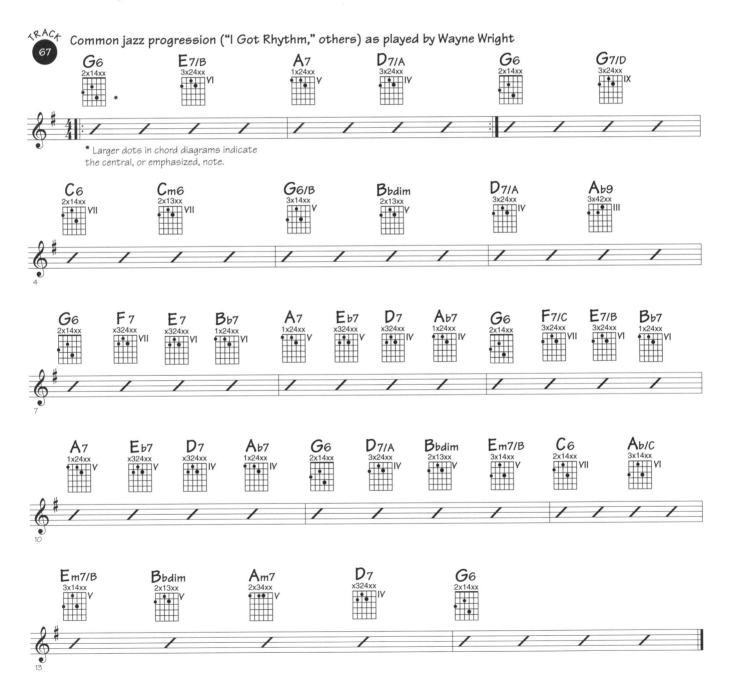

Common jazz progression ("I Got Rhythm," others) as played by Wayne Wright

TRACK 67

The sound of the acoustic archtop is essential to the job. "[Jimmy] D'Aquisto told me that this type of guitar," said Wright, tapping his rare, left-handed D'Angelico, "was designed to sound from the third fret to about the tenth. You lose some down here [*he played a low note*] and you lose some up here [*he played a few high ones*]—it's right here [*he played a few punchy midrange chords*].

"And the sound's got to decay fast," Wright went on. "When you're playing rhythm, you've not only got to feel like the drummer feels, you've got to *feel* like he feels! You've got to feel the way he feels about the length of the beat. It ain't that much; it's like a chirp. Otherwise you can't get that pulse."

Like Berliner, Wright was struck by Freddie Green's extraordinary projection. "When I was with Buddy Rich back in the '70s," he recounted, "they had a tribute to the guy who did all the booking for everybody. So Freddie Green came in and sat down to play [with the Basie band]. There was no mic near him, but when I listened to the tape the next day, the first thing that came through was that damn guitar!"

Apparently Green was canny about acoustics beyond his guitar, too. Wright recalled, "I saw Freddie at a record date with the Basie band, sitting there, and I said, 'Where the hell's the mic?' Again, no mic near him. What he had found out to do was find a sweet spot in the room that sounded good to him, and that's where he sat."

AL GAFA

I first heard guitarist Al Gafa at Windows on the World, atop New York City's World Trade Center. As I approached the room where the drumless piano trio was playing, I was intrigued to hear what sounded like the top end of a trap set ringing out. Entering the room, I realized it was Gafa, chopping out chords on his Gibson Johnny Smith, the volume rolled way back, as the bass player soloed.

"In that situation, I was playing like a drummer and also trying to get the high-hat feeling going on two and four," said Gafa. "Sometimes you can't really hear the chord because I'm choking it off to get that rhythm."

Gafa is a versatile player. He toured extensively with Dizzy Gillespie, and his work with singer Johnny Hartman was featured on the soundtrack of the film *The Bridges of Madison County*. He's not a traditionalist, but he has thoroughly absorbed the principles of rhythm playing and applies them where he sees fit. And regardless of what he's playing, the unamplified voice of his instrument is his touchstone. "No matter how loud the music gets, I try to get the acoustic sound of the instrument to come through," he said. "I use the amplifier only to get presence.

"I try to find the thing that works best," Gafa continued, "whether it's full electric or a trio job. My voicings are based on the section I'm sitting in, but I can always hear the acoustic instrument itself. Strings are important," he added. "I use a .013 high E down to a .054 bass; you get more projection."

When I asked Gafa to play something, he surprised me with the '60s hit "One Note Samba" by Brazilian Antonio Carlos Jobim. His highly syncopated up-down picking was a clean departure from the four-to-the-bar downstroke swing style, but with its clear voice leading, percussive attack, and muting, it was a beautiful adaptation of the traditional approach. "It's the old technique," said Gafa, "but it also sounds like a Latin percussion instrument."

"One Note Samba" as played by Al Gafa
Tuning: D A D G B E

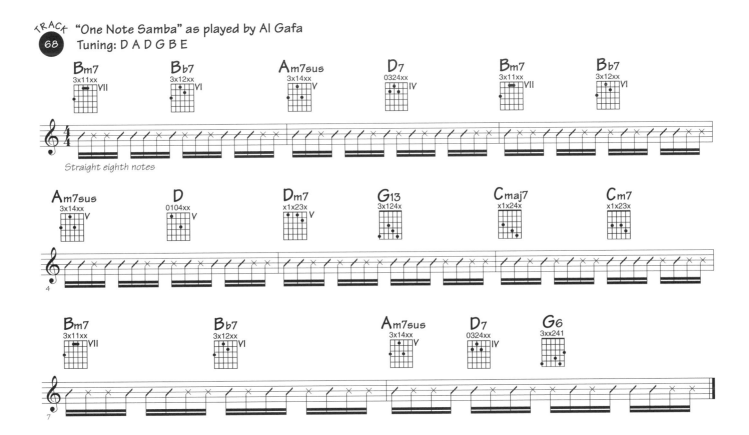

Straight eighth notes

an introduction to gypsy jazz

Michael Simmons

Django Reinhardt.

In the late 1920s young musicians all over Europe were struggling to master the new music from America called jazz. Although many of them managed a credible copy, a Gypsy guitarist named Django Reinhardt was the first European to go beyond mimicry and forge an original jazz style. The music he and violinist Stéphane Grappelli made with the Quintet of the Hot Club of France had such an impact that musicians around the world still play the string swing they created in the '30s.

Django Reinhardt was born in Belgium in 1910 and was raised in typical Gypsy fashion—with lots of music and plenty of travel. His mother, a dancer, and his father, a violinist, wandered through Europe and North Africa with Django and his younger brother Joseph in tow, following a thousand-year-old tradition.

The Romany Trail begins in India, the birthplace of the Gypsies, and ranges through the Middle East and into Europe and North Africa. As the Gypsies passed through new villages and towns, they discovered that they were as valued for their music as they were feared and reviled for their strange and unfamiliar customs. When they arrived in Europe in the 14th century, the local populace thought they were magicians from Egypt and eventually the name *Egyptian* was corrupted, in English, into *Gypsy.* In France they are called the Manouche, in Spain the Gitanos, in Germany the Zigeuner, in Italy the Zingari. They call themselves Roma and their language Romany. Over the centuries the Gypsies developed a powerful instinct for survival and they have a saying that reflects a hard-earned knowledge: "Stay there where they sing; evil people would have nothing to do with songs."

In Paris, a city that loves songs, the Gypsies found a ready home. After World War I, the Reinhardt family settled in the encampments that had formed on the outskirts of the city. The young Reinhardt soon made a name for himself backing up accordion players in the local dance halls on the guitar-banjo. He played a style called *musette,* a form of waltz that came to Paris from Auvergne in the 1860s. The music took its name from the musette, a small bagpipe on which it was originally played. By the turn of the century, Italian immigrants had replaced the bagpipe with the accordion, and Gypsy guitarists soon added their distinctive rhythmic touch.

Reinhardt proved to be a prodigy. At the age of nine he won a dance-hall contest, and by the time he was 13 he was a full-time professional. In 1928, at the age of 18, he made his first recordings on guitar-banjo with Jean Vaissade and soon after with Victor Marceu. These recordings, once believed to be lost, were rediscovered a few years ago. The record companies had a difficult time deciding how to spell the young Gypsy's name. On the Vaissade discs he is called Jiango Renard, and Marceu settled on Jeangot. While the recording quality is not particularly good, these early efforts show that Reinhardt was already a remarkable guitarist, as he echoes the rapid accordion arpeggios with his trademark rhythmic flourishes.

But Reinhardt's promising career almost ended before it began. On November 2, 1928, he returned home late from a job at a club called La Java. His caravan was full of celluloid flowers that his pregnant wife had made to sell the next day at the cemetery. While investigating a noise, he accidentally dropped a lighted candle into the artificial flowers, which burst into flame. Reinhardt was able to get out of the caravan, but his right leg and left hand were badly burned.

He was rushed to the hospital where doctors wanted to amputate his leg. He refused, and his friends moved him to a nursing home where he started a painful 18-month convalescence. Whenever his mother asked him what he was thinking about, he replied mournfully, "my hand." One day his brother Joseph brought him a guitar in an attempt to boost his flagging spirits. With a remarkable display of will, Reinhardt struggled to teach himself to play guitar with his mangled hand. Contrary to all expectations, he relearned to play and emerged from his convalescence a better guitarist.

After his recovery, Reinhardt and his brother Joseph returned to their old haunts to play music. It was around this time that Reinhardt heard some records that were to change his life. In 1931 the brothers were playing in cafés in Toulon, in the south of France, when they met a painter named Emile Savitry. Savitry had just returned from

Reinhardt with Rex Stewart, Duke Ellington, and members of the Hot Club.

SELECTED DISCOGRAPHY

There are many excellent reissues of Reinhardt's music. Unfortunately, specific titles tend to go in and out of print with surprising frequency. Most recordings of the original Hot Club are excellent. Recordings with visiting American swing musicians like Coleman Hawkins and Ben Webster are interesting in that they show how Reinhardt's Gypsy style compares to the American swing style. Later (post-World War II) recordings with a standard rhythm section of piano, bass, and drums (and occasionally with Reinhardt playing electric guitar) often contain some incredible, mature playing but don't illustrate the string swing sound as well as prewar sides. The French label Fremeaux is slowly releasing everything that Reinhardt recorded. As of this writing they have put out ten two-CD sets and they are only up to 1940. Here are a few things to look for.

DJANGO REINHARDT

Djangologie, Vol. 1, DRG 8421.

Djangologie, Vol. 2, DRG 8424.

Djangology 49, RCA/Bluebird 9988.

Django with His American Friends, DRG 8493.

The Indispensable Django Reinhardt, 1948–50, RCA 66468.

Verve Jazz Masters, Vol. 38, Verve 16931.

The Complete Django Reinhardt, Vols.1–10, Fremeaux 301–310, Fremeaux, distributed in the U.S. by FTC Distribution, 8306 Wilshire Blvd. #544, Beverly Hills, CA 90211; (310) 327-4243.

DJANGO REINHARDT AND STEPHANE GRAPPELLI, WITH THE QUINTET OF THE HOT CLUB OF FRANCE

Django Reinhardt and Stéphane Grappelli, Pearl Flapper 9738.

First Recordings, Original Jazz Classics 1895.

Souvenirs, Verve 20591.

Stéphane Grappelli, Reinhardt, and Lucien Simoens.

America with some records of American jazz musicians, including Louis Armstrong and Duke Ellington. When he heard Armstrong's horn for the first time, Reinhardt held his head in his hands and wept. This was the music he would play for the rest of his life.

In the summer of 1934, he was hired by Louis Vola, a musician he met in Toulon. During the breaks he started jamming with a violinist named Stéphane Grappelli. That autumn, inspired by the string jazz of Joe Venuti and Eddie Lang, Django, Grappelli, Vola, and guitarist Roger Chaput started a quartet. Joseph Reinhardt joined soon after, and the Quintet of the Hot Club of France was born. Before long, the Quintet's music was being heard around the world. American jazz musicians visiting Paris began to seek Reinhardt out to jam. He made records with players like Benny Carter, Bill Coleman, Eddie South, and Coleman Hawkins. He was even invited to tour America with Duke Ellington. In 1934 Reinhardt started playing a new guitar designed by Italian luthier Mario Maccaferri and built by the Selmer Company. The Selmer guitar had a bright, percussive attack much like the banjo but with a warmer tone that suited the swing that Reinhardt was now playing. He would play Selmer guitars until he died.

After the war, swing jazz was eclipsed by bebop, and audiences began to lose interest in prewar styles of music. Although Reinhardt continued to record, producing some of his finest work, he was increasingly seen as an anachronism. Older members of his audience only wanted to hear the old Hot Club standards, such as "Swing 42" and "Nuages," which the younger crowd dismissed as old-fashioned music. But when he started playing in a more beboppish style on electric guitar, he was derided by both his old fans and the young Turks for trying to cash in on the latest trend.

Both groups had it wrong though. Reinhardt's later electric playing shows that he *was* listening to the new sounds from America, but he was fusing bebop with his Gypsy sensibilities and creating a new style. Unfortunately he died of a stroke in 1953 and was never able to bring this more introspective, less frenetic music to a wider audience.

Gypsy Guitar Primer

John Jorgenson

RHYTHM

The best place to begin in learning Gypsy guitar style is with rhythm guitar. Gypsy jazz rhythm is similar to the archtop rhythm guitar style of such players as Freddie Green and Eddie Lang (in fact, Lang was one of Reinhardt's early influences); it's not really a barre-chord style. The chords move around so quickly in Gypsy music that you don't have time to go to a full barre chord.

One of the most useful chords you can learn for this style is this minor-sixth shape:

The minor sixth is characteristic of Gypsy music; in Latin, jazz, or swing music you'd tend to use a minor seventh, but in Gypsy music you use a minor sixth most (but not all) of the time.

Let's look at the song "Minor Swing," which has three basic chords (Am, Dm, E7). You start with the minor sixth with the root at the fifth fret, then move that shape up to the tenth fret and you've got a Dm6, then take it back down three frets to the seventh fret and you've got an E7 (with the fifth in the bass).

Gypsy jazz can be an overwhelming style when you first hear it, so take it a little at a time.

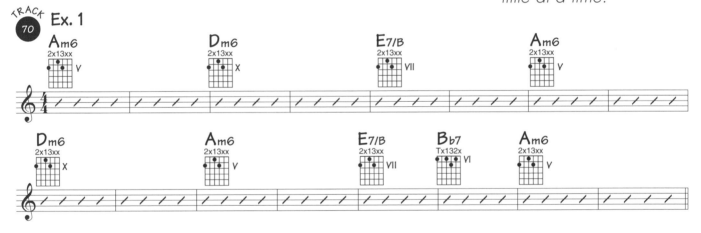

If you were playing "Sweet Georgia Brown" in the key of F, you could start with that same shape at the fifth fret, but now it's going to function as a D7. Move it up to the tenth fret and you've got a G7, go down to the third fret for a C7, and finally play an F chord in first position like this:

Introduction

As you can see, the minor sixth shape is very useful; it can serve as a minor sixth, seventh, diminished, or flat-five chord (if you consider the bass to be the third).

WALKS

Django Reinhardt actually started out on the six-string banjo, so a lot of his chording techniques come from the banjo, which has no sustain. The basic idea is to keep harmonic motion happening. It's similar to bluegrass bass runs, where instead of sitting on a G forever, you throw walks and runs into other chords.

In "Minor Swing," you can walk from the Am6 up to the Dm6:

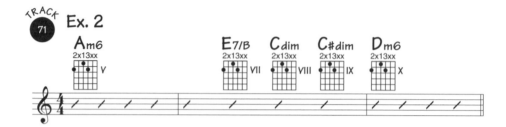

Here is another useful walk for a tune like "I Got Rhythm." Start with the F chord shown earlier, then play that minor sixth shape at the second fret to make an F# diminished chord. After that, play a Gm7 at the third fret, then go either to a minor-sixth shape at the third fret for a C7 with the fifth in the bass, or a normal C7 chord.

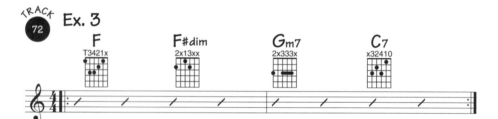

If you want to go from an F chord to a B♭, as in the bridge of "Honeysuckle Rose," you can begin with your F chord in first position, go to our minor-sixth shape at the third fret, and then move that shape to the fourth fret. From there the shape expands, with the middle and ring fingers moving up a fret while the index finger stays on the third fret, forming an F/A chord. Then end on a B♭6 chord.

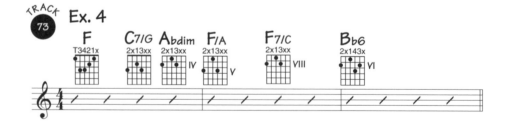

STRUMMING

In a band context, the bass is going to be playing strong on beats 1 and 3, so the guitar needs to accent the 2 and 4 to make it swing. Play a percussive ghost strum on the bass strings on beats 1 and 3 followed by a strong, full strum on beats 2 and 4. You can also throw in a quick upstroke on the upbeats after the accented 2 and 4 (1, 2 *and* 3, 4 *and*).

LEAD LICKS

What I've found while learning Reinhardt's solos is that there is a lot of motion up and down the neck, I think because he was only working with two fingers. It's not based around boxes like blues. One of the main building blocks for his lead style is the diminished seventh arpeggio. Practice playing this pattern up and down the neck. The example below (starting at the third fret) can be used in the key of Gm or in the key of F or Fm over the V7 (C7) chord.

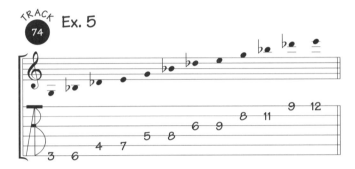

Example 6 is a diminished run you could use over a D7 moving to a Gm chord. Playing these notes over a D7 chord actually implies a D7b9 chord. This shape can also be moved anywhere on the neck to play in different keys. (Remember to play all of these examples with a heavy swing rhythm.)

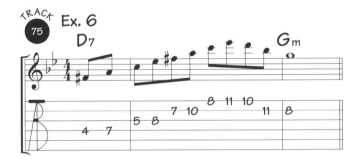

You'd use the following run over a C7 chord moving to an Fm. Notice that the first two notes of the triplet are played with consecutive downstrokes.

This passage in the key of C, from "Swing Guitar," combines a lot of different elements.

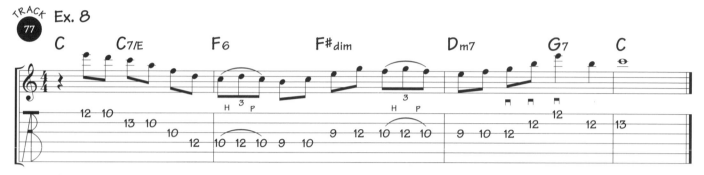

Use Example 9 over an F7 going to a Bb, or a Cm going to a Gm.

Here is a *huge* chromatic run that Reinhardt often used. He would usually go across the strings chromatically until he reached the high E string, where he would run it all the way up, fret by fret, with one finger.

Reinhardt used a lot of sweep picking licks (notes played with consecutive downstrokes). Here is an example from "Minor Swing."

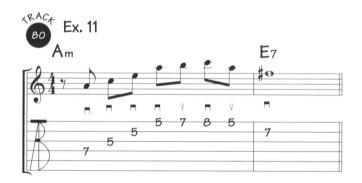

Here's a run to play over an Am or D7, using the same first three notes of the last lick.

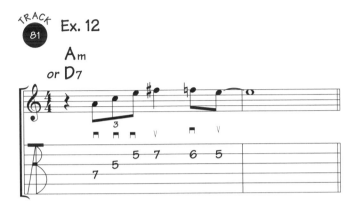

Reinhardt also used open strings often. This is an open-string lick from "Minor Swing."

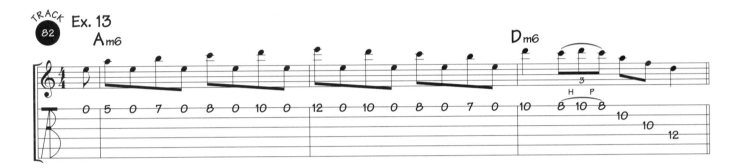

Here is a cross-picking lick similar to one Reinhardt played in "Appel Direct."

That should be plenty to get you started. Gypsy jazz can be an overwhelming style when you first hear it, but just take it a little at a time. Start with one tune and pull it apart, then move on to another. If you keep doing that, pretty soon you'll see the patterns emerge and understand how they fit together.

Inside a Django Reinhardt Solo

Scott Nygaard

Learning complete solos gives you a sense of how to shape your own solos.

Most guitar instruction these days is oriented toward the micro—learn these two-bar licks, learn this scale that works over this chord, learn that one-measure pattern. But before the flood of instructional material that began in the '70s, many musicians learned to play by learning the solos of their mentors. And they didn't just learn the few measures that contained their favorite licks; they learned whole solos. Legend has it that when Wes Montgomery first started performing, he was limited to playing the Charlie Christian solos he had copied from records. He couldn't even play rhythm guitar at the time. He would simply lay out until it was his turn to solo and then launch into one of Christian's solos. Whether this is true or not, it could have been, and it was undoubtedly true of other musicians, both novices and soon-to-be-legends. In addition to gaining a good grounding in the vocabulary of whatever style of music they were interested in, learning complete solos gave musicians a sense of how to shape their own solos and how to use rhythmic variations that might not fit neatly into two- or four-measure packages. It also made them realize that natural melodic flow was more important than theoretically correct note choice.

Let's look at a solo Django Reinhardt played on a recording of his Gypsy-jazz standard "Minor Swing." It's one of Reinhardt's more popular tunes, in part because the melody and chord structure are simple enough for beginning swing soloists to handle and in part because the simplicity of the chord structure leaves a lot of room for rhythmic and melodic invention. While examining the details of Reinhardt's ideas, we'll concentrate on how he structured his solo and see how he manages to sustain interest over 64 bars.

Recorded in 1949 (Reinhardt's "late period"), the solo begins with a gorgeous, fluid, four-bar line that outlines the Am and Dm chords. If you heard only this line without the accompaniment, you could easily guess what the chords were. It is followed by another four-bar line that does the same thing over the E7 and Am chords (measures 5–8). These lines include some interesting harmonic extensions: the inclusion of the ninth in the Am arpeggios (the B note in measures 1 and 8) and the sixth in the Dm chord (the B note in measures 3 and 4), which in concert with the third (the F in measure 5) foreshadows the E7♭9 arpeggio in the next two bars. But what Reinhardt is really *doing* here is giving the listener (and his bandmates) an authoritative, driving introduction to the tune.

Part of the charm of much of Reinhardt's music is the chugging forward motion achieved by both the soloists and the rhythm section, and Reinhardt puts the entire band right in the pocket with these eight bars. The transition between soloists is often an unsure rhythmic time in small bands, especially if the soloist is also an important component of the rhythm section. Most soloists have a slightly different approach to time and often may unconsciously begin their solos at a slightly different tempo than the previous solo. These eight bars taught me that it is wise to begin solos in a strong and unambiguous way so that the rhythm section can lock in behind you.

Once the groove is taken care of, a little space and a nifty off-beat rhythmic variation is in order. Notice how Reinhardt takes an odd little four-note phrase (measure 9, which stresses the major seventh of the Dm chord) and alters it to fit the next chord (measure 11) but places it in a different place in the measure. He then slips into another fluid line over the E7 chord that ends with a B♭7 arpeggio superimposed over the E7 (measure 14).

Minor Swing

Music by Django Reinhardt and Stéphane Grappelli

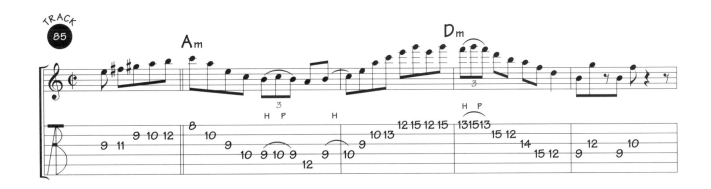

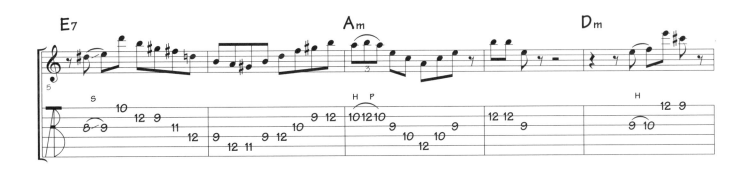

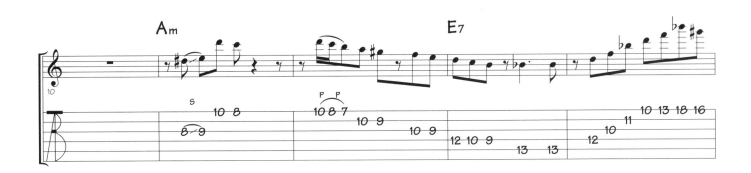

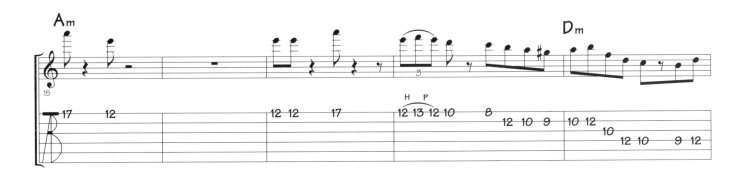

© *Francis Day Publications. All rights for US controlled by Jewel Music Publishing Co., Inc. Used by permission.*

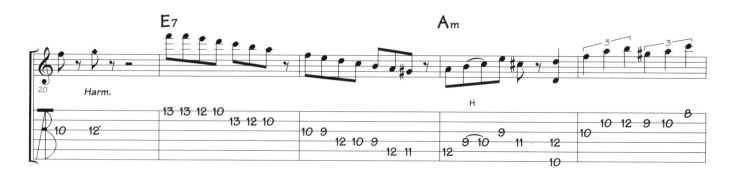

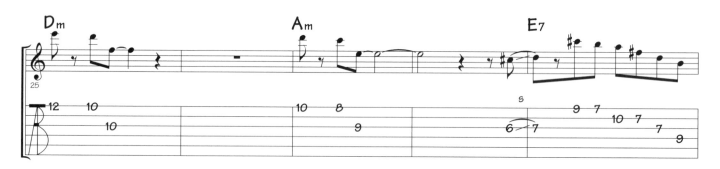

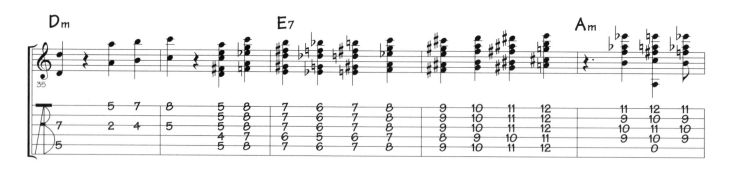

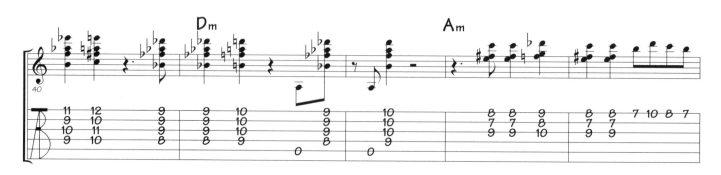

This is a common harmonic substitution in bebop, and Reinhardt illustrates how to do it gracefully and dramatically. This line reaches the 19th fret on the E string, so it may be difficult for guitarists whose instruments don't have cutaways, but it's a useful idea that could be transposed to another key for another tune. Notice how he is beginning to extend the harmonies in these eight bars: he outlines a DmMaj7 chord and then plays a B♭7 over the E7 chord.

Reinhardt continues to expand the harmonic possibilities in bars 23 and 24. In bar 23 he implies an A7 chord, which leads into the Dm, but notice that he has gotten to the Dm chord five beats early. Anticipating chords is common in bebop and is a way to make it appear as if the backup chords are being played in reaction to what the soloist is playing rather than the other way around (as an invariable harmonic structure to which the soloists' melody must strictly conform).

The phrase in measures 29–30 could be said to be a mistake. Reinhardt plays a Bm7 (or E13) arpeggio that includes a strong C♯ note. This would be a strong line if we were in the key of A (file this phrase away as a iim–V7 lick in a major key), but it is certainly not a recommended choice for the key of Am, which is, of course, defined by a C♮. But listening to the solo on record, nothing seems out of order. Although it is not a particularly inspired note choice, it does illustrate that rhythmic flow and phrasing are just as important as book-perfect lines. The line neatly finishes off the solo, despite the "mistake." In fact, try substituting a C♮ for the C♯ and it just won't sound right. Go figure.

Measures 33–44 increase the intensity with a figure in octaves (measures 33–35), a series of chromatically ascending ninth chords (measures 36–38), and some syncopated punches on minor sixth chords (measures 39–45). Reinhardt follows these chordal flourishes with another fluid line that dips and dives and features one of his signature crab-walking diminished arpeggios (measure 46).

The next section begins to cool off a little. Measures 49–54 feature a nice little riff that could easily be the seed of another tune. After giving us something we can hum, Reinhardt slips back into some perfectly timed arpeggios outlining the chords that echo the way he began his solo. He also ends unambiguously, as if to say, "That's what I have to say about that."

After dissecting the details, it's important to look at the whole solo. Reinhardt begins with a solid line that outlines the harmony and gives us a good strong groove. He then begins what might be called "variations," although not in the strict *theme and variations* sense. What he is varying is the harmonic content of the underlying chords and the rhythmic phrasing, offsetting phrases by single beats and entire measures. He then increases the intensity with some octave and chordal flourishes. At this point he is about three-quarters of the way through, and his solo has reached its peak. In the last quarter he cools off and ends with a repetition of the harmonic outline with which he began way back in measures 1–8. This basic structure is just one of many approaches to soloing, but it is one that is very common in swing and bluegrass (and all of their hyphenated variants). It's also a very effective approach for short solos in songs (as opposed to two-chord jams).

Learning entire solos like this can take a lot of work. It requires patience and good ears (see "Learning Songs Off Albums," *Acoustic Guitar,* August '98). Writing the solos down is a good idea, because even if they contain licks you can't play (which happens more and more as you begin learning solos played on different instruments), you can still learn something by analyzing them. It is a very rewarding exercise and will greatly expand your concept of soloing, no matter what kind of music you're interested in.

DISCOGRAPHY

**Django Reinhardt,
Djangology 49, RCA/Bluebird 9988.**

an introduction to texas swing

Hal Glatzer

One evening about 50 years ago in Denison, Texas, an aspiring guitar player went to a dance to hear Bob Wills and the Texas Playboys. Wills' guitarist, Eldon Shamblin, had developed an innovative style to back up the fiddling, and young Royce Franklin was so impressed that he copied it and showed it to his fiddle-playing father, Major Franklin.

At first, father and son played "San Antonio Rose" and other Wills songs, but then they applied the technique to traditional hoedowns and breakdowns like "Gray Eagle," "Sally Goodin," "Crafton Blues," and "Beaumont Rag." Royce and his younger brother Ray eventually developed something original on their flattop guitars: a strong "boom-chuck," with the "boom" a walking bass line and the "chuck" a strum of fundamental and passing chords. Their right-hand attack was a punchy, emphatic sock that gave fiddlers a solid foundation over which to swing.

Without being entirely conscious of it, the Franklins were finding a groove that had much in common with what swing and jazz guitarists were playing on archtops in those years—the 1940s—as rhythm players in big bands (see "Freddie Green's Rhythm Style," page 55). And they also sounded a lot like the guitarists backing up Django Reinhardt and Stéphane Grappelli in Europe at the same time, though the Franklins never heard the Quintet of the Hot Club until many years later (see "An Introduction to Gypsy Jazz," page 60).

SELECTED DISCOGRAPHY

Matt and Danita Hartz (featuring the Franklin Brothers), *Texas Fiddle.* Royce and Ray Franklin play backup on separate channels. Available from County Sales, PO Box 191, Floyd, VA 24091; (540) 745-2001; fax (540) 745-2008; www.countysales.com.

Barbara Lamb, *Tonight I Feel Like Texas,* Sugar Hill 3860.

Mark O'Connor, *Championship Years,* Country Music Foundation 015. Recordings of O'Connor's live National Fiddle Championships competitions, 1975–84.

Mark O'Connor, *Soppin' the Gravy,* Rounder 0137. Includes O'Connor on rhythm guitar and Jerry Thomasson on tenor guitar.

Benny and Jerry Thomasson, Voyager 309, cassette only. Voyager, 424 35th Ave., Seattle, WA 98122; (206) 323-1112.

Bob Wills, *Anthology 1935–1973,* Rhino 70744.

Bob Wills, *Tiffany Transcriptions,* Vols. 1–9, Rhino 71469–71477.

Bob Wills and His Texas Playboys, *For the Last Time,* Capitol 28331.

Various artists, *Texas Fiddle Favorites,* County (out of print). Features Major Franklin on fiddle, backed on guitars by his nephew Louis Franklin and Norman Solomon.

The Texas Playboys back in Tulsa.

Omega Burden, Major Franklin's friend and frequent guitar accompanist, was also intrigued by the new style. But where the young men played what Royce still calls "clamp chords" in up-the-neck inversions, Burden preferred more open, ringing chords; where the brothers used chromatic bass runs, he kept his bass lines closer to the tonic and fifth notes of the chord, as an upright bass player would.

What they had in common, of course, was the powerful right-hand sock that cleverly complemented swing fiddle. With the help of that rhythm, much of the Appalachian repertoire moved into new musical territory, finding young audiences of swing dancers across the western states during the 1950s and '60s.

Burden later added more closed chords to his backup work, but there remains to this day a stylistic spectrum over which Texas swing guitarists range. The extreme ends are in two other styles that blossomed in the '40s: chord-melody jazz (see "Beginning Chord Melody," page 27) and straight-ahead bluegrass. Most players are in the middle, but with leanings one way or the other.

Texas Swing Backup

Hal Glatzer

Texas swing is fun to play, and it's not inherently difficult; the rudiments are well within the reach of intermediate guitarists. Getting good at this style opens up arrangement opportunities: besides hoedowns, country and western, and cowboy songs, there are many old-timey, ragtime, bluegrass, Tin Pan Alley, and swing-era melodies that can get a new lease on life over a Texas-style backup.

And working your Texas swing chops all the way up to perfection can be profitable. Guitarists who play it right are in great demand as accompanists in fiddle competitions, not only in Texas but all over the West. At Weiser, Idaho, where the Grand National fiddle championships are held every year during the third week of June, those backup guitarists who get on stage most often and take home "favorite accompanist" awards traditionally receive ten percent of the prize money the contest-winning fiddlers get.

Texas swing is almost always played on a flattop, often a large Gibson or Epiphone. The Gibson-style instruments tend to produce consistent volume across all of the strings, whereas the comparably large Martins may favor either the high strings or the low strings—or both—to the detriment of the notes in the middle. With a couple of exceptions, Texas swing guitarists use fairly heavy picks on medium-gauge strings.

THE RIGHT HAND RULES

"I don't really have a style; it's just what I do with my right arm," said Royce Franklin. "My dad was always strict in the timing, and I learned that no matter what chords you want to put in, you've got to keep to the rhythm. In this type of music, especially on stage, you may be the only guitar player with the fiddler, and your right arm makes all the difference. Once in a while, though, if the fiddler gets a bit off, you can hit a backstroke and bring him back. It helps to keep him from running away or getting out of kilter."

"Royce doesn't get wild with his right hand," concurred fellow guitarist Rex Gillentine. "He plays progressive enough to be interesting, but not so progressive as to be out in left field." Gillentine went on to explain that Franklin's take on the rhythm was passed down from the source. "If you listen to people who grew up with the style, if you sit at the feet of the people who invented it, modified it, and made it what it is today, then you know you're getting it from the people who have that style ingrained in them."

That's what Gillentine did too, and he's been playing for 30 years. "I've never been to Weiser, but I have a room full of trophies," he said, "and I've played in Nashville with - [fiddlers] Johnny Gimble and Mark O'Connor."

As Gillentine put it, "The guitar work is almost a little song in itself, but it was invented as a complement to the progressive style of fiddling. It's a bass-wise progression, predicated on the moving bass line with a chord following each note. You could hit an open G chord with the G on the sixth string in the bass and then hit the same chord using the B on the fifth string in the bass. But in this style, we might use that B note with a G9 or a G7 chord.

Since many backup progressions are built on closed chords, they can be moved up the neck easily.

Introduction

G9/B

G7/B

"The beat is hard to describe, but I like to grab onto a barre chord and make that thing ring as long as possible before I change to the next chord, and not damp it off. You're striking that chord for a purpose—to be heard. It won't be heard if you use your guitar like a snare drum."

LEATHER BRITCHES

According to Gillentine, "'Leather Britches' is a stock tune, but one with a good progression. It's a good tune to start on because this arrangement works with the bluegrass or old-timey version, if that's what your fiddler knows." The music at the top of the next page shows the melody and a basic, straightforward backup. Get comfortable with it before tackling the other examples. The first variation replaces one of the D7 chords with a D/E chord (D with an E in the bass) in measure 7.

The second variation starts and ends with a full barred G chord. You may want to mix and match comparable measures from several of the other variations. For example, measures 7 and 8 in the first variation can substitute for measures 7 and 8 in variation 2.

Variation 3 really walks up the neck. In the fifth measure, the single-string notes are down-picked and are given equal weight. The final G chord is a closed-position C-chord fingering. Notice how, in all these variations, the final tonic chord is an up-the-neck inversion rather than a first-position chord. Like never hitting the same bass note twice in a row, ending high on the neck is very characteristic of the Texas swing style.

Texas swing players almost never use capos. But since many backup progressions are built on closed chords, they can be moved up the neck easily. Try taking variation 3 up two frets to the key of A for tunes with the same progression, such as "Gray Eagle" and "Sally Goodin."

Leather Britches

Traditional, backup as played by Rex Gillentine

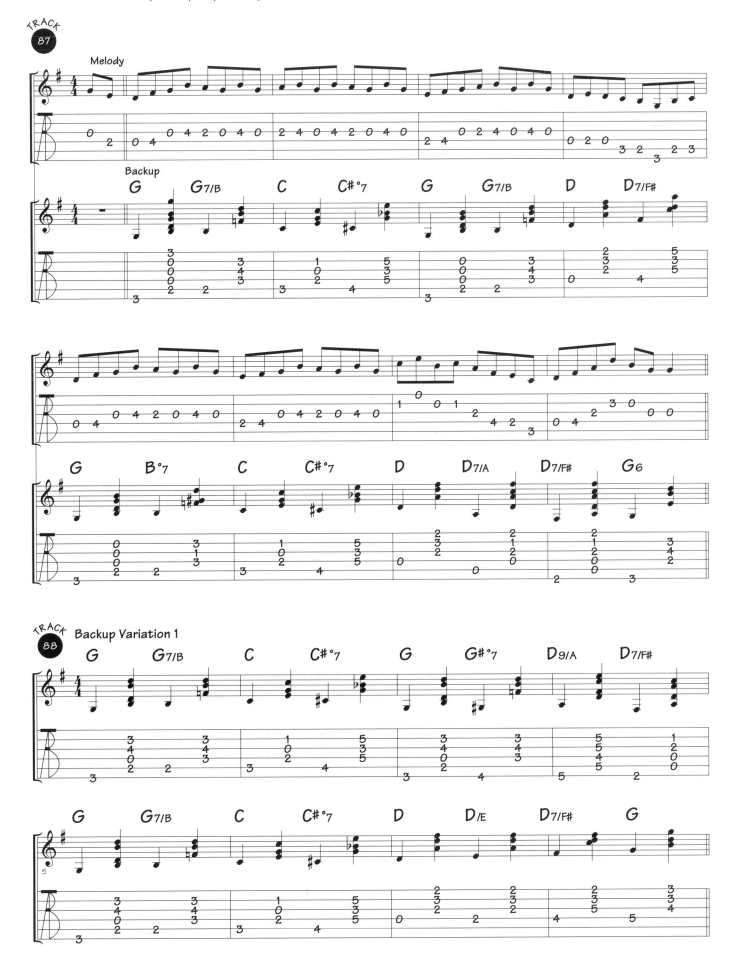

Subscribe & Save $66.88!
3 Convenient Formats, 1 Low Price.

WANT TO IMPROVE YOUR GUITAR TECHNIQUE? Read our lessons in the magazine and listen to the musical examples on the Web.

SHOPPING FOR GUITARS AND GEAR? Read what our experts have to say in the magazine and watch their online video demonstrations.

ADDING SONGS TO YOUR REPERTOIRE? Take advantage of both print and Web to get the songs, and the background on the artists who create and interpret them.

You'll receive *Acoustic Guitar* 12 times a year … enjoy 24/7 access to www.acousticguitar.com … and between issues, you'll get fresh news and alerts via email with *Acoustic Guitar Notes.*

If purchased separately, you'd pay $91.83. Act now, and your one-year subscription is just $24.95, a savings of 73%!

1 *Acoustic Guitar* in print, 12 times a year.

Through *Acoustic Guitar* magazine's renowned interviews, reviews, workshops, sheet music, and song transcriptions, you'll learn music from around the globe and get to know the artists who create it. Our product reviews and expert advice will help you become a smarter buyer and owner of acoustic guitars and related gear. And our advertising pages will acquaint you with the amazing spectrum of people and companies who serve our global guitar community.

2 *Acoustic Guitar All Access.* Available 24/7!

Visit www.acousticguitar.com—named among the "Best of the Web" by *Forbes* magazine—and you'll arrive at the number one online destination for acoustic musicians and enthusiasts. A small sampling of our Web content is free to the public, but the best is available only to subscribers like you: with *Acoustic Guitar All Access,* you get 100% of our premium, Web-only audio and video lessons, reviews, interviews, and other features, plus the amazing archive of articles and stories from our print edition, and participation in Web forums, giveaways, and other events.

3 *Acoustic Guitar Notes,* your monthly e-mail alert.

When *Acoustic Guitar Notes* arrives in your inbox on the third Wednesday of every month, you'll know there's a healthy dose of guitar bliss ahead of you. *Notes* brings you the latest guitar news and alerts you to the newest audio and video lessons and reviews available to you through *Acoustic Guitar All Access.*

Subscribe Right Now!

A whole year of *Acoustic Guitar* in three great formats is just $24.95, saving you 73% off the regular price.

Fill out and mail the postage-paid reply card opposite. Call toll-free, (800) 827-6837. Order online at www.acousticguitar.com/subscribe

Get expert guitar instruction with more titles from String Letter Publishing

COMPLETE ACOUSTIC GUITAR METHOD

Book and 3 CDs
136 pp., $24.95
HL00695667

FINGERSTYLE BLUES SONGBOOK

Book and CD
40 pp., $9.95
HL00695793

ACOUSTIC GUITAR FINGERSTYLE METHOD

Book and 2 CDs
80 pp., $24.95
HL00331948

FLATPICKING GUITAR ESSENTIALS

Book and CD
96 pp., $19.95
HL00699174

FINGERSTYLE GUITAR ESSENTIALS

Book and CD
88 pp., $19.95
HL00699145

SWING GUITAR ESSENTIALS

Book and CD
80 pp., $19.95
HL00699193

ROOTS AND BLUES FINGERSTYLE GUITAR

Book and CD
96 pp., $19.95
HL00699214

ALTERNATE TUNINGS GUITAR ESSENTIALS

Book and CD
96 pp., $19.95
HL00695557

ACOUSTIC BLUES GUITAR ESSENTIALS

Book and CD
72 pp., $19.95
HL00699186

ACOUSTIC GUITAR CHORD & HARMONY BASICS

Book and CD
72 pp., $16.95
HL00695611

ACOUSTIC GUITAR SLIDE BASICS

Book and CD
72 pp., $16.95
HL00695610

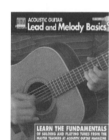

ACOUSTIC GUITAR LEAD AND MELODY BASICS

Book and CD
64 pp., $14.95
HL00695492

ACOUSTIC GUITAR SOLO FINGERSTYLE BASICS

Book and CD
64 pp., $14.95
HL00695597

ACOUSTIC GUITAR ACCOMPANIMENT BASICS

Book and CD
64 pp., $14.95
HL00695430

SONGWRITING & THE GUITAR

88 pp., $14.95
HL00330565

BLUEGRASS GUITAR ESSENTIALS

Book and CD
72 pp., $19.95
HL00695931

INSIDE BLUES GUITAR

88 pp., $14.95
HL00330757

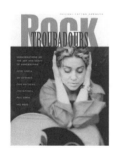

ROCK TROUBADORS

192 pp., $14.95
HL00330752

At your music or book store, or order direct • Call (800) 637-2852 • Fax (414) 774-3259
On-line at www.acousticguitar.com
Hear about our newest titles by subscribing to our free Acoustic Guitar Book Report e-newsletter
at www.acousticguitar.com/forms/enewsletters/